SIMPLY IMPOSSIBLE, IMPOSSIBLY SIMPLE

*How a seemingly impossible
project came into being
through childlike faith*

Janice V Paskin

malcolm down
PUBLISHING

Reader reviews

Janice open-heartedly shares with the reader her experience of obeying God's call to create a place for the healing of hurting and broken lives. She is captivatingly honest about her tears and tribulations as well as the waves of hope and extraordinary breakthrough that propelled her onwards when it was tempting to give up.

Janice's personality emerges from the pages in a most refreshing way. She writes spontaneously and with great character, insight and kindness. I love the way she shares meaningful Scriptures all throughout her book, describing in very practical terms how she applied them in particular situations. As I read, I could feel my spiritual roots growing deeper – nourished by the testimony of someone who loves Jesus with a passion and has learnt to lean into Him and trust Him every step of the way.

This book demonstrates, so very beautifully, that – when we walk closely with God – there is *always* provision for the vision, however impossible it might seem.

ANN SHAKESPEARE, Author of *God's Gift of Tremendous Power*

A breath-taking journey and testimony to God's faithfulness and His Kingdom principle of seed, season, fruit and harvest. It has been a privilege knowing Janice and Norman and learning something of what God has done in and through them in this season. A hard to put down read . . . I wait with great expectation for the next glorious chapter in their lives and ministry . . .

LOUISE MARSH, Founder The Evergreen Care Trust

Honest, compassionate, faith-filled, and determined, these are some of the qualities of Janice and Norman Paskin. I am honoured to call them friends. Janice's story in particular is one of an open-hearted willingness to let God transform her life, and then use her to transform others. This book is an honest, heart-felt read that encourages us to let God have His way through all of life's challenges and believe that we really can do what He says we can do when we put our hands into His, and join Him in the adventure of faith. Set time aside and read the story…you won't regret it!

JONATHAN CONRATHE, Founder and Director of Mission24
Author of *Radical Christianity* and *The Power Partnership*

If you feel that God has a plan for your life (which He does) but feel stuck or frustrated or confused, or you need fresh faith and inspiration, then this wonderful book will help you immensely. There is so much gold in here to both inspire and instruct anyone in their journey of faith, especially if you feel you're facing one challenge after another. Janice and Norman are two of the most encouraging and inspiring people I have ever met. From the first time we met them as they welcomed us into KingsGate, through over 20 years of receiving personal encouragement from them again and again, to observing this amazing story unfold, theirs is a story that needs be told.

This one tells you something of their outrageous, tenacious and unstoppable faith; of the blessing of being connected into the family of God, and above all of what God can do when ordinary people set themselves to hear from Him and won't let go until He comes through as He promised. Read it and be encouraged!

SIMON DEEKS, Executive Pastor and Centre Overseer KingsGate Community Church

What a pleasure to read this story of faith, truly encouraging! Summarised by one of the guest's feedback the essence of this work could be encapsulated by the words 'I feel refreshed! Such a non-judgmental place that I felt an instant sense of belonging.' Whether it is through a person or a physical space could these words be a small reflective light of Jesus' physical ministry on earth, that those looking toward him (with all humanities cracks and frailties) were warmly welcomed closer in full acceptance.

Janice writes of her lack of qualifications and openly tells of worries and fears within this challenging venture. But, through a constant turning back to God in a humble and resilient faith, seeds of hope have been planted in the lives of many.

To do anything great, we need people around us and Janice writes so well the importance of this. With the amazing support of her life friend and husband Norman, and the many people she looked to for support, prayers were lifted up and time and time again this is a story of how God answers.

To play a small encouraging part in The Well Head Centre and Healing Rooms and read this story in print has not only encouraged me but I am confident will encourage others. The ministry of Jesus found connection in people's lives as bridges of changed realities complimented His words. These changes are clearly evident over the years and as you read through, I am confident you will find a joy and warmth from the stories inside.

Janice, well done and may you see many blessings realised for all your service. It's hard to pull a book together, but in sharing this story let the seeds you have sown continue in the encouragement of others to follow the dreams and visions God has placed within their hearts.

STEVEN PETTICAN, CEO Light Project Peterborough

ISBN 978-1-915046-58-1

Layout and editing by Helen Jones

Contents

Acknowledgements

Here are some of the people, churches and organisations I would like to thank for making this project possible. There is no way that I could repay them for all they have done in this project, but I know for sure that they will get their reward.

My husband, Norman – Always there for me
Philip Warner (Warners Printers) – for his generosity, support and willingness to allow us the use of his property.
Warners Maintenance Team
Mark Renshaw
Gill Renshaw
Gerald Johnson
Ann Hopkins
Graham Tickle
Mary Williams
Godfrey Birtill
Graham Stannard
Pete Kelly
Amanda Johnson
Alison Quinlan
Catherine Quinlan
Bourne Baptist Church
KingsGate Community Church
Bourne Life Group
The WOW Team from KingsGate Community Church
Josh Peters
Sovereign Landscapes
Network Peterborough

Stringers of Bourne
Branch Bros Market Deeping
Peter Hubbard
Peter Dawson
Bourne Interior Furnishings
Fitzgerald's Beds
Simon Wilson
Mickey Vincent
Brent Warner
Phil Burrow
Margaret & Brian Gray
Tricia & Roy Smith
Porcelanosa Peterborough
Scholes Funeral Services
Keith & Beryl Griffiths
Alan Myson
John Bufton
Sue Nott
David & Gill Mabey
Simon & Zia Deeks
The Salvation Army, Bourne
Our faithful Trustees
Our faithful Volunteers
All those 100+ on our Prayer Support Team
All our faithful (monthly) Financial Partners

All of my family and friends who have supported and encouraged me along the way, especially Linda Martin when I had discarded even the idea of carrying on with my book and bringing it through to completion. I shall be forever grateful. Bless you, Linda.

This is the scripture that has kept me going. I read it every day to encourage me to keep doing what I am doing.

*'I will go before you and make the crooked
places straight;
I will break in pieces the gates of bronze and cut
the bars of iron.
I will give you the treasures of darkness and hidden
riches of secret places,
That you may know that I, the Lord, who call you
by your name, Am the God of Israel.'*

Isaiah 45:2-3

Crisis point

Extracts from the author's diary 1992–1995

I am struggling with feeling low and don't know the reason why. I have lost my joy and can't seem to turn things around. It's been going on for longer than I can say. I am always trying to put a brave face on things, but my family knows there is something not quite right. I just can't pretend anymore. I can't keep putting on an act. My family have to put up with my behaviour as I sometimes have to go off to cool down many times. Sometimes I just need to get away from everybody and be on my own. It doesn't seem to help much either, but I have to try something. When we are having our evening meals together, I sometimes feel that I can't engage in the conversation. It is like I could hear what they are saying but cannot understand it. I am there in body but not in spirit. They haven't done or said anything wrong, so it is quite difficult for us all at this time.

I have a very good friend who says I can pop round anytime for a chat but I know that she is struggling with some medical issues of her own so don't want to burden her with my problems.

The family are all doing well with our son Glyn just going off to university in Coventry and our daughter, Hazel, at the grammar school here in Bourne. Church seems to be fine too. The fact that life's normal activities are going well makes it even more difficult for me to understand why I'm struggling so much.

I work part time as a receptionist at the local dentist in the town. It is a very busy practice and I enjoy meeting all our patients and don't feel I have any issues there. I don't have any time to think about myself whilst at work as there are always patients to deal with, which is good! This is a bit of normality for me.

At 7pm this evening after I finish my shift I plan to head off into the night and not return as Norman is not able to pick me up this evening. I have had enough. At 6.45pm, Norman calls me. 'I'm back home now, Jan, and can pick you up after all. See you in a few minutes.' Sighing heavily, I let the phone drop on the receiver. I am not happy. I thought I had it all planned. A way out, or so it seemed. Things are coming to a head, and I need to get some professional help.

I am now seeing two counsellors and I seem to be counselling them! I also have a Community Psychiatric Nurse assigned to me, but this isn't working either. My visit to the GP has resulted in him putting me on anti-depressants. I don't really want to go on them, but I have decided to take only half the prescribed dosage. My friend has told me of a retired Salvation Army Officer who is a professional Counsellor and a University Lecturer, so I have booked an appointment with him to see if that works.

I have just come out of my first session, and I think it went quite well. I have been given some homework to do before my next appointment. He is so understanding and kind, so lovely to talk to and a very good listener. We will meet again next week. Today I didn't need the full hour as he had cracked it! Yippee! I am back to my old self. I am laughing and enjoying life once again.

I will be forever grateful to my friend and her counsellor friend who found the key to my healing. It seems depression can creep up on you when you least expect it. And during that painful time in my life, I could **never** have foreseen that all I went through would be used – powerfully – to help others in similar situations.

Introduction

Let me introduce myself. I am a 68-year-old grandmother of five. I have two grown up, married children. I live in a small market town in Lincolnshire called Bourne. At the age of nineteen in September 1971 I got married to Norman, and we both now attend KingsGate Community Church in Peterborough, Cambridgeshire. Having left school at fifteen with no qualifications, I just had a heart for the hurting and broken and knew I would have to do something about this sooner or later!

In 1995 when I had recovered from the depression, I realised that God was wanting to use that time for His Glory. Fifteen years earlier I remember praying a very dangerous prayer! I do this from time to time. I was meeting so many broken and hurting people during my ministry times in church and I said to God, 'How am I supposed to help these people if I haven't experienced such pain for myself!' Well, guess what? He let me experience it for myself, didn't He?

As I was going through that awful time, I realised that there seemed to be nowhere for people to go to get away from their situation and just talk to someone who would be willing to listen. It haunted me for years after I was well. I knew that God was speaking to me about a place of healing. I wasn't sure how all this would come into being, but I knew something would happen which would involve healing hurting and broken lives. I held this in my heart for about fifteen years. It emerged every now and then. I kept asking God to show me when, where and how this would take place.

He had put it on my heart to open a Centre for those struggling with the pressures and stresses of life like I had experienced. People like me who didn't know where to go to get the help and who to talk to. A place to go where I didn't know the people and to get my head straight so I could try to get things back into some sort of order in my life. I would have travelled anywhere to find the right place for me. Distance didn't matter. No pressure, just people around me who want to listen and love me. That's all I needed. All I needed was some time and space in the right environment.

That is now what we offer to all our guests who come into The Well Head Centre and this is my story.

Planting an acorn

In January 2008 I knew I had to take a break from heading up the Welcome Team at KingsGate Community Church, Peterborough. I had been Head of Welcome for about ten years along with my husband Norman. Being Head of Welcome meant that we were responsible for the oversight of nine teams (totalling around eighty volunteers) which included Car Parking, Stewarding and Welcome every Sunday covering three services. It was quite stressful and time consuming as we had to organise all the rotas and meet up with team leaders during the week. So, I asked if I could have a month off, to which the Leadership Team kindly agreed. After my month was up, it didn't feel right for me to carry on doing it. I felt God was trying to get my attention and I needed more time to spend with Him, not knowing what was about to happen. After talking to Norman, he agreed for me to step down but said that he would continue to head up the team for the moment.

Six months later, I had the opportunity to go to Lakeland, Florida for a Todd Bentley Healing Conference with four ladies from our church. We had a wonderful time. We were all prayed for many times by various people. I was told that everything I touched would turn to gold and that I would get everything I asked for, and I knew then what God was asking me to do. (At least I thought I did!)

We received a fresh anointing whilst we were there, and we all brought the fire back to our localities. When I returned to Bourne, my son and daughter-in-law told me that a lady at the Baptist Church, which they attend, had also just come back from Lakeland, Florida, and she was on fire for God too, and perhaps we should get together to talk about it. So, they gave me her phone number and we started meeting every Wednesday afternoon for prayer. Her name is Alison.

Alison is a mighty woman of God. She is a qualified Primary School teacher and is married to Niall and they have four children. She told me she always wanted to open up a Healing Rooms and I told her that I always believed that God wanted me to run a Residential Centre for the hurting and broken in our society. The depressed and oppressed were on my mind too. We thought that God had put us together for a reason and we would pray until He revealed more to us.

In early November I went to a conference in Dudley with Alison and two other ladies. Whilst I was there, I saw gold dust on my hands for the first time. I had an overwhelming urge to ask someone to pray with me about giving up my job at Charles Read High School, near Bourne, where I was a TA (Teaching Assistant). This had been on my heart to do, but I just didn't know when was the right time. During the worship time, I began experiencing pains like those when you are in labour, I said to Alison, 'I feel like I am giving birth to something.' It was really strange. I have never felt anything like this before, except when giving birth to my children, and certainly not in a meeting! I remember seeing other people writhing about in meetings before, but I never thought that one day I would be doing that. After the meeting on the Saturday afternoon, I plucked up the courage and went forward to ask the Pastor of the church at Dudley to pray for me, to help me make my decision. After he had prayed with me, I felt a release to hand in my notice as soon as I got home. I had settled something in my spirit that this was what I had to do, whatever the circumstances. Whatever happened I had to do it! After that I was so exhausted, I sat down and closed my eyes, as they were hurting. Whilst I was resting, God gave me a picture of some bungalows that I knew about in Bourne that were empty. They had been boarded up for some time. I went past them every time I walked into town. I jumped up out of my seat and went straight over to Alison and told her what God had showed me. I said they were the Manor Lane bungalows that used to be residential housing for adults with special needs. She hadn't heard of them until I said they were called St. Peter's bungalows. Then she said, 'That is it!' God had been saying to her St. Peter's, but she didn't know where or what that was as she hadn't lived in Bourne long. So, we decided to go and find out who they belonged to as soon as we could.

* * *

The following Friday, Alison and I went to have a look around the outside of the bungalows just to see if they were fit for purpose, and whether they matched my vision. We had a good look round. They were a bit dilapidated, but we were not perturbed. The next thing we needed to do was to find out who owned them. As we were walking away from the bungalows, we noticed a planning application sign attached to a lamppost. It read that Mr Warner (the Managing Director of the printing company next door to the bungalows) had applied to the Local Council for permission to change the bungalows from residential accommodation to offices. We knew then that we had to contact Mr Warner. Alison said, 'You do it Janice!' So, I phoned up Warner's Printers in Bourne and asked for Mr Warner. When the receptionist asked, 'Which Mr Warner do you want?' I was stumped as I didn't realise there would be more than one! She then said to me, 'There is Steven and Philip,' so I just went for the first one and said 'Oh let's go for Steven,' so she put me straight through to Steven Warner. I said to him that he wouldn't know me, but would it be possible for me to have an appointment with him to talk about the Manor Lane bungalows. He said, 'I can't help you with that, it is my brother who deals with them; would you like me to get you transferred?' So, I was immediately transferred to Philip Warner and repeated my request. Philip then arranged for Alison and me to meet with him face to face on Monday 15 December at Warner's Printers to discuss our thoughts further. I couldn't wait!

When I handed my notice in at the school, it went much better than I expected. A few people cried when I told them, but that was quite nice to see (in a funny sort of way!). My line manager (Mary) and the Head Teacher plus a few others who I worked alongside, asked me what I was planning to do, so I told them what I felt God was leading me to do. We now wait and see what takes place from this day of decision.

The staff were are all very pleased and supportive of the vision I had received. That evening, I went to a party at the PE teacher's house and one of the other TA's told her that I was leaving and so she came over to me and wanted to know everything, and so I told her. She wanted to help us in any way she could too. It seemed every person I told was very excited for me. I told my hairdresser, friends at church, family members, friends in Bourne, staff at school and I got very positive reactions from them all. It was all very encouraging.

My church friend Mary in particular was so excited about it all and offered to pray for us the following Tuesday evening when the four of us, that is Alison, Niall, myself and Norman were getting together to pray about us meeting up with Mr Warner. I told Amanda who also offered to pray for us. Not only that but she said she would come with us if we wanted her to. I was bowled over by this as she knew the Warner family well. Other friends also offered to pray for us during the meeting.

* * *

At the beginning of December, I met another friend in Bourne, a powerful lady of prayer, and she was so excited about the project. The words of the song –

'Though none go with me, still I will follow,
Though none go with me, still I will follow,
Though none go with me, still I will follow,
No turning back, no turning back.'

– kept coming into my mind and thoughts, which reassured me that I may have to go it alone sometimes, even though God would never leave me. Others may not have the same passion and commitment as me, but that's OK.

'Trust in the LORD with all your heart and lean not on your own understanding, in all your ways acknowledge Him, and He will direct your paths'. Proverbs 3:5-6

We met together with Alison and Niall to talk about and pray together about our vision and dream, and the bungalows in Manor Lane and had a great time discussing God's plans.

It occurred to me what a momentous task I had taken on, but a plan was starting to come together. My friend Sue phoned me with some good advice. We needed to gather a committee. People of like mind. Professional people. People of influence and integrity. Aided by intense times of prayer and fasting, lots of people were expressing an interest in our project and it felt like things were starting to come together.

Alison came round and we had a chat and a prayer time together. We fasted today too and Amanda joined in with us at home.

Two days before I left Charles Read High School, the PE teacher gave me a lovely rose bush called 'Happy Retirement' as a leaving gift. She asked me all about our new venture and was very interested in it all. She promised to let me know of places, people and agencies that we can contact regarding financing it all.

The same day we had our appointment with Philip Warner. Amanda had a track of Godfrey Birtill playing in her car. It was called 'Fertile Ground.' It made me cry. We believed it was God speaking to us about the land we were about to possess.

Philip seemed a little apprehensive to begin with. He said he didn't think he could help us but as the conversation went on and we had had time to share our vision and dream, I believe God melted Philip's heart and he became more interested. He told us afterwards that he thought we were going to complain to him about the bungalows and that he had had many complaints about the buildings being left unused and youths had been in and made an awful mess. At one point there was a stunned silence and I thought 'What I am doing here? Beam me up Scottie!!' I asked Philip if he would like to think about our proposal over the Christmas period, talk it over with his family, friends and work colleagues, and then perhaps we could come back and meet with him in the New Year. He said that in the New Year when we come back, he would show us round the bungalows. With that we assumed that he would now let us use the bungalows for a short term as we figured he wouldn't show us round the bungalows and then say 'well here they are, but you can't have them' would he?

We booked another appointment in the New Year where all three of us would go back and see what he had come up with. When we came out and were getting into my car on the car park, we all believed that we had sown a seed that day and it was going to blossom and grow into something beautiful for His Kingdom. That night Alison went to a prayer meeting and one of the guys said he had a word for someone there. He said, 'An acorn has been sown today and will grow into a beautiful Oak Tree.' He didn't know what we had done that day, but Alison did, and she told him that that word was for us. How amazing is that? We believe that was God just confirming to us that we were on the right track. In the evening I went to our TA's Christmas Meal at Grantham. We had a great time, and I was presented with a beautiful cyclamen and some vouchers to spend at a Garden Centre. Another TA asked me what I was going to do when I left. I told her what was in my heart and she was thoroughly flabbergasted!! She did say that I had it in me as I was a good listener and very thoughtful and kind to people. Apparently, it was my thing! I had to say a small speech at the end of the evening, and so I told them what stage we were at, and they were all very pleased for me and wanted to be kept informed of every step along the way.

Wednesday 17 December was my last day at school. It was hard at times, especially when one of my pupils was uncontrollably crying. He was so upset that I wasn't going to be there anymore. He was one of my librarians. I had a chance to talk to many teachers and others about what I planned to do next. I said in the staff briefing that God had got me the TA job, and now I believe He has given me a new vision to move on to.

Three friends of mine have said individually that they believe Mr Warner will let us have the bungalow for a 'peppercorn rent'! I didn't understand what that meant but friends said that it means 'next to nothing', a very low or nominal rent!

We had our small group social at our house this evening. We were all very excited about the events so far and looking forward especially to the New Year and all that unfolds.

Two days later, Norman and I went to Alison and Niall's for a Christmas Party. It was great, and we had a chance to talk together. Alison told me that she had had the chance to talk with Chris (the one who gave the word in the prayer meeting) and he gave her some more words of encouragement to add to the first. He said something about the polluted water would be purified again. Alison felt that God had told her that there would be no tares growing up, no weeds. I took it to mean God would not allow anyone or anything to disrupt what Alison and I have a vision for. I felt sure there would be people who would like to add their own ideas to the Healing Centre, but we needed to be careful in all that we undertook for Him. It's His vision and His purpose that we were fulfilling. This was another sign and confirmation which increased our sense of excitement.

The next time we went to church, Amanda said to me, 'It is a done deal, it is ours.' I chatted to Keith and Beryl Griffiths who were really keen to offer any practical help we might need when setting up and other people offered to pray for the situation over Christmas. People were all for us, and for the vision we have. It was tremendous.

All was quiet over Christmas and we prayed for God to be at work in Mr Warner's life.

We've got it!

Early in the new year, Amanda felt confident that the buildings were ours. She had had a prayer time recently and was confident that the Warner family would want to be part of our dream for Bourne and, when we next meet Philip, he would be more than happy to help us in any way he could.

We began to draw up our 'Short, Medium and Long Term' plans so we could present them to Philip Warner on our next visit.

Alison and I prayed over a map of Bourne and booked an evening meeting on 29 January in The Jeans Café to lay out our vision and dream for Bourne to anyone who might be interested in either intercessory prayer for the project or ministry on the Healing Team.

I phoned Philip Warner today to book another appointment with him. We are now booked in to see him on Tuesday 20 January. That is Alison, Amanda and myself to have a chat with him. He said that he would get the keys and show us round the bungalows. He was so really lovely!

A church friend expressed her willingness to help in The Healing Rooms during the day on the Healing Team. She was part of The Healing Rooms in Peterborough so she would be a good help for our team. Another couple were happy to help too, both practically and with prayer support. Amanda decided not to come along with me and Alison on the 20th to see Philip Warner as she was having a day with her son and granddaughter. What she did say was 'It is done, we have it.' This increased mine and Alison's eager anticipation.

On Tuesday 20 January, we went to visit Philip Warner with regards the bungalows. He offered us coffee on arrival this time. Philip has offered us one of the bungalows FOC, FREE OF CHARGE. We only needed to pay for bills such as electricity, gas, water and phone bills etc. We were on cloud nine! It seemed that Philip was just as excited as us as he wouldn't stop talking! He planned to draw up a formal agreement so we would all know where we stood and what was expected of us. He did mention that in the lease he would need to refer to the FOC as a 'Peppercorn rent'. When he said that, I nearly jumped up and gave him a kiss! [Why? Because you remember, three of my friends individually prophesied that this would happen!]

Despite the bungalow needing lots of work to get it ready for occupation, we could do it. We would keep in touch over the next two weeks and then get together with Philip after that to sort out all the finer details. He said he had chatted it over with his family during the Christmas period and they were all in agreement with letting us use the bungalow. He even said that it was his wife who had said to him, 'What have you got to think about Philip; let them have it!' We told Philip that we were praying God's favour on him and his business and he replied, 'Well I don't want to upset your boss then, do I?' He was so funny. God is so awesome. We looked forward to the next two weeks and to the time when Philip gives us the key.

Shortly after this, I was reading 1 John 5:14-15:

'Now this is the confidence that we have in Him, that if we ask anything according to His will, He hears us, and we know that He hears us. Whatever we ask, we know that we have the petitions that we have asked of Him.'

The truth in His word reminded me of the power of God's promises over our lives and gave me confidence that they would be fulfilled.

When Alison and I met to discuss our next steps, she mentioned having told her prayer group of our plans and two of the ladies said that they had been praying about these bungalows for many years. Inevitably, they were absolutely 'gob-smacked' when they heard this good news. They had been praying that God would use these bungalows for His Glory. In addition, Ann Hewitt had a dream about the bungalows which included an acorn and the oak tree.

The day before Alison and I met to discuss our next steps, I read Isaiah 61 again and I believe God gave me a new revelation in His word. Normally I skipped through this chapter, missing chunks out, but that day I read it all slowly and was truly amazed. All that is in it applies to us at this moment in time as well as prophesying the way it will be in the future. God is so good. Every line is wonderful news to us, our families, the next generation and the nations. I texted Alison to encourage her to read the passage. Alison texted me back to say that a friend of hers had a picture of many people in chairs, and we had the keys to unlock these chairs. This scripture was amazingly accurate and I believe it is for us, Bourne and beyond at this time.

On Thursday 29 January, we had our meeting at The Jeans Café to inform as many people as possible in Bourne, and to let them catch the vision we had been given. Quite a few people came, but there were lots who didn't turn up for various reasons.

Alison talked first about setting up the Healing Rooms and had compiled a leaflet unpacking our vision. After a break, I spoke about the wider vision of a Healing Centre. At this point I felt a bit like Moses in Exodus 4:10 when God had asked him to speak, and he came up with all the reasons why he couldn't do it. But I knew I had to do it, and I knew that God would be with me. I spoke of when I first felt God speaking to me about a Healing/Care Centre in 2001. I was shocked at how far back it was myself as I had imagined it was about 2004, but I found an entry in one of my journals and there it was in black and white. I was so pleased I had bothered to look back to check!

We had a very encouraging question and answer time at the end. There were just a couple of people who had reservations about what we were about to undertake, but on the whole, it was mainly positive and we would proceed. At the end of the evening when most people had left, Alison asked me if I had got any gold dust on my hands. When I looked down, I saw sprinkles of gold on them and my heart leapt. Just then, Sue Fitzpatrick (a friend from church) said, 'You had it on your face earlier.' I'm not sure what this means but I know it is a sign from God that we are on the right track and He is with us. I've not seen this before so I am just feeling my way around it and trusting

God to reveal to me His plans and purposes in all this. Sometimes I don't even know it is on me until someone tells me. Around this time there were people in our church receiving gold teeth!! I think we just need to trust Him in all things.

Norman suggested we have an Open Day and invite the local churches to come and see the bungalow so they could catch the vision too and help bring it to fulfilment.

The following day, I met up with Janie (one of the Pastors at our church) and had a great time chatting over coffee at one of the cafés in Bourne. She was so excited for us, for Bourne and the lives we would impact. She gave me lots to think about and pointers along the way. That was very helpful to me. She offered to pray for a name for the centre and encourage others to as well. Janie said she was so pleased to see me looking so happy and excited and that I had waited a long time for this. She said I would be telling others about this and encouraging them not to give up on their dreams. I told her that I had never heard God speak to me so often nor seen things so clearly before. Now my eyes were truly open and my ears unblocked too. After she had gone, I jumped on the bus to go into Peterborough as I wanted to get some moisturiser from Boots.

On the bus I was listening to Jill Austin on my iPod. She was wonderful. She really inspired me to go higher. I felt the Lord was bringing me back to the parable of the talents where the man who received only one talent did nothing with it. He just buried it in the ground. Jesus ordered his talent to be taken from him and given to the one who had ten. Verse 29 of Matthew 25 says this:

'For to everyone who has, more will be given, and he will have abundance, but from him who does not have, even what he has will be taken away.'

I believed God was encouraging me that because I had been faithful in little things and was now using the gifts and talents He had given to me, He would give me more. God was truly at work. I was hearing more, discerning more, being more confident, trusting God more, expecting God to show up more, believing for more and not shocked when it all worked out His way. He had gone before me and made the crooked places straight, and I was thrilled that His timing is always perfect and it is NOW. I had been waiting and waiting for this for years. God is so faithful.

That same day, Norman spoke to a guy from church who was willing to help with anything that he could do, and he would pass on the information to all the groups in his circle of influence. People were so up for it. I could hardly keep up with it all!

In early February, Alison forwarded me an email from Philip Warner. He seemed to have come up with a problem and said that he would let us know if he could sort it out in the next eight weeks. If possible, then we could have the bungalow for five years on a lease. We believed the bungalow was still ours, so I contacted everyone who I knew would be praying for us to get them all praying for this unexpected situation. We had a group of dedicated people who would not give up and would only settle for God's best.

I had an amaryllis plant in my kitchen and I had been excitedly watching it grow since planting it just before Christmas. I wondered what colour it would be. Well, it grew very tall and one of the flowers burst open and was pale pink. Two of the buds dropped off. I was not happy about that, but then I saw a double shoot on the plant coming up by the side of the other one, so I began praying for that one to blossom fully with four flowers on it. If it did, this would be such an encouragement. The Lord frequently speaks to me through nature, especially flowers, and I believed He wanted to speak to me through this amaryllis. As I saw the other bud coming up alongside, I know that all will be well with securing the bungalow. It would take a little longer than we anticipated but everything would turn out right in the end.

The next time I met with Alison to pray, we discussed praying about a new name for the Healing Centre and prayed for a dynamic 'Prayer Team'. We also prayed for Philip Warner to give us even more than we asked for when he comes back to us in eight weeks. We wanted to receive God's best in this and believed God would turn it all around for His glory and honour.

On Sunday 8 February, I went to help out at the final 'Welcome Lunch' at our church, KingsGate Community Church. Things were about to change within the Welcome Department at the church and, as I was there at the beginning, Mike Pawson (one of our Pastors) thought it would be nice for me to be at the last one too. I was put on a table with Norman and lots of people sat chatting. I started talking to a lady called Sue who was also with her daughter and three granddaughters. She also worked as a TA (another one!) at that time, and so I told her that I had just left school as a TA and what I was about to embark on. She was so thrilled and wanted to be part of it with me. She lived with her daughter in Wittering, on the RAF base. When I told her we were going to have a Healing/Care Centre in some bungalows she said, 'I have been seeing three bungalows with lots of grassy areas and trees, large trees.' Would you believe it? The bungalows are next to a park where there are lots of large trees. I told her about the acorn and the oak trees, and she said she had a cross-stitch tapestry of an oak tree, which she was going to give to her mother, but she died, so she would give it to me. She also told me that I am a sower. After the meeting, I emailed her the vision I had and how it has come to be so far. I'm sure meeting Sue was a God appointment and He had great and wonderful plans for Sue and her daughter in our centre.

On the 16th February, Alison, Niall, Norman and I met to have a chat and a prayer time together. We urged each other on and not to get discouraged in any way about the delay. It was all in God's timing.

The next day, we went to a Ministry Training Evening at our church which was led by Rachel Hickson. At the end of the evening, she and her friend Helen who came with her, wanted to prophesy over a few people, and they picked Norman out.

Helen said, 'You are going to see things come into fruition that have been a long time coming. It's like you've planted over many, many years and sometimes it's been slow to see any fruit and to see the effect of your labour. He is actually saying to you, you are going to see a big harvest in the days to come. It's like God is saying to you, "Come on

Norman, let's go and explore this new territory because it's a much bigger field than you imagine.'" You can't imagine what a thrill went through me as Helen said these words.

Then Rachel put a hand on Norman's shoulder and confirmed Helen's words: 'I just see the field of healing and it's just like there's healing houses growing up and very fruitful trees. I see healing in the nations too. God says it is time! It is time!!'

Norman and I sat quietly, holding hands and drinking it all in. We knew we were in God's perfect plan and timing for each of our lives, and there would be a great harvest. Praise God.

God revealed to me in a dream that we would need people to stay overnight in the Centre, so there would be 24/7 cover in the place. I saw Keith and Beryl (from our church) coming one day, staying overnight and going back the next day. I thought, well that seems a possibility! Nothing is impossible with God, so the next time I saw Keith, I put it to him, and he was in total agreement with what I had said, and he said he would be up for it. Accordingly, I believed God will prepare others to offer their time and their services to the Centre in this way too, so that it could be manned 24/7. God is in total charge, and He was revealing bit by bit what could be achieved there.

Over the course of the next few weeks, I received a series of confirmatory scriptures from other believers and through my own Bible reading. One key verse was Luke 1:14, which said,

> 'Blessed is she who believed, for there will be a fulfilment of those things which were told her from the Lord.'

Although this was about Mary, the mother of Jesus, Amanda and I took this as a word from the Lord for us. Another key passage came from Isaiah 58:12, in the Message Bible:

> 'You'll use the rubble of past lives to build anew, rebuild the foundations from out of your past. You'll be known as those who can fix anything, restore old ruins, rebuild and renovate, make the community liveable again.'

I also took this as an encouragement for our journey with the healing centre.

Also, Amanda phoned me one morning to give me the scripture from Psalm 105:19:

'Until the time of His word came to pass.'

We must never give up and think God is not doing things on our behalf. He is preparing everything, getting everything in place. We need to trust Him completely to finish the work that He has begun. Praise His Name.

I believed He spoke to us at that time to keep our spirits up, and not get downcast as we waited for Philip Warner to get back to us. We had two more weeks to wait!

That same day, Amanda had the scripture Luke 10: 8–9 which says:

'Whatever City you enter, and they receive you, eat such things that are set before you, and heal the sick there, and say to them, "The Kingdom of God has come near to you."'

Just two days later, we received the email that we had been waiting eight weeks for. Philip Warner would let us have the bungalow FOC, FREE OF CHARGE until 2013. This was such an encouragement, as we could begin moving forward with our plans!

One morning in early April, I woke up with the right side of my neck and jaw in pain. Initially, I didn't understand why. Then I remembered what Paul Clift said at the Healing Rooms training we went to, that sometimes God puts things on us as a word of knowledge for someone else. So, I wrote it down and gave it to Norman to take on Sunday morning to church. The Bible exhorts us to ask the Lord for words of knowledge for people who need healing in the services each week.

When I arrived at church the following Sunday, I wanted to speak to Mary B. When I found her, she was talking to Rob from our worship team who had just been talking to her about his mouth and neck hurting for the last few days after visiting the dentist. She said,

'He needs prayer. Janice, will you pray for him?' When I asked him what he needed prayer for, I nearly burst! You know, God is so good. I prayed for him in the Welcome Area. Later in the morning at the end of the services, Janie (one of our Pastors) told me three people had responded to that word of knowledge. That really encouraged me.

After the church meeting, I caught up with my friend Sue. We had a great time together. Whilst we were praying, she had a picture of a wooden bowl which was beautifully made, but empty. I believe God was showing both her and me, that He wanted us to be empty vessels for Him – vessels of honour, handcrafted by Him. Wooden bowls as He is the Master carpenter. We both laughed and then cried together. He was bringing us together. He was putting the right people across my path and preparing all of us for the task He had set before us.

On Tuesday 21st April, we had our appointment with Philip Warner. Before we went, Alison, Amanda and I had a prayer time together and the Lord gave us a scripture and a picture. The scripture was Isaiah 45:2-3:

'I will go before you
And make the crooked places straight;
I will break in pieces the gates of bronze
And cut the bars of iron.
I will give you the treasures of darkness
And hidden riches in secret places,
That you may know that I, the Lord,
Who call you by your name,
Am the God of Israel.'

We prayed and asked God to reveal to us what were the treasures of darkness? Then we got the reply. All those who are bound by Satan were the treasures of darkness. They were the ones He would give us. They were the ones whom He would set free. Amanda had a picture of a baby being born and we believed that new life would be birthed in that place.

Our meeting didn't quite go as I thought it would. I hoped we would be signing on the dotted line for the bungalow with Philip passing the key over to us so that we could go in and get started on the project. However, Philip gave us a plan of the bungalows and told us that he was only letting us have one of them at this time, and that is No. 12. On the plans it is a large bungalow with thirteen bedrooms and two bathrooms, one extra toilet and two store rooms, one kitchen and a sluice room. We brought the plans home with us to consider how we can best utilise these rooms and then we would need to go back and have another look inside the bungalow to see if we could make it work as both Healing Rooms and a Care Centre.

Philip told us that we might need to contact the Council to find out whether we needed to request a 'Change of Use.' So, as soon as I got home, I went online and filled in the necessary form and submitted it to South Kesteven District Council (SKDC). We had no idea how long this would take but we were trusting in God and standing on His promises.

Feeling a little deflated by the obstacles, I remembered the picture of the new-born baby and sensed that represented where we were at that moment in time. What does a new-born need? Not much! A cot, a room and some clothes. It doesn't need four bungalows to live in! As it grows, it will need so much more. So, as our Healing Centre needed to grow, we believed Philip would release more of his bungalows to us. We would start small and build up. This reminded me that God was in total control and I left it with Him.

In the evening, I went to a Ministry Training Evening at church and Diane Webb prayed for me. All that she said just confirmed that He is in control. I was doing what He wanted me to do. I was taking new ground. I was faithful and obedient and He was pleased with me. I was not to give up.

Shortly afterwards, I was reading Isaiah again, and got to chapter 61 verses 7 to 11 (in the Message version) where it says:

'Because you got a double dose of trouble and more than your share of contempt, your inheritance in the land will be doubled and your joy go on forever.'

I claimed it for the bungalows here in Bourne. I claimed it for the land and the people of Bourne and surrounding areas. We would get what God has planned and destined for us, and no man (or devil) could stop it. I also claimed again Isaiah 45 verses 2-3 (see above).

In early May, I phoned SKDC to see if they had any information for us regarding the planning application. They told me that we would need planning permission to use the bungalow as a Healing Room, but not as a Care Centre. It would cost us £335 for the process with no guarantee of a positive outcome! So we would wait, pray and see. The application process could take at least eight weeks.

One Sunday morning as I was having my quiet time, Amanda gave me a call and had some wonderful news for me. I had given her a book to read called *The Treasures of Darkness*, which I had bought on Amazon, as we were desperate to know what the 'treasures of darkness' were that we read about in Isaiah 45. She felt that the Lord was telling her that the 'treasures of darkness' were people with mental illnesses, and that the Healing Rooms would be known as a place of healing specifically for the mentally ill, the oppressed, the depressed, those with no hope, those whom others didn't know what to do with. We discussed this for over forty-five minutes. It was great, and we felt it was so right for Bourne.

That same evening, I went to a 'Closer to God' meeting at the Baptist Church, and we had a prayer tunnel to go through whilst people prayed over us from different sides. There were many encouraging words spoken over me at that time. Things like 'You are going to see things you have never seen before, things here in Bourne.' Also, Colin Pratt had a word where I was compared with Ezra and Esther in the Bible. The King granted Ezra all he requested, and Esther received favour from the King too. I received that as a specific word from the Lord for me.

On Monday 11 May I phoned SKDC again to have another chat with Rob about the 'Change of Use' for our Healing Rooms/Care Centre. I told him that we would be opening a Residential Care Centre for the vulnerable and hurting in Bourne, and The Healing Rooms would only be open a few hours per week. As the premises were originally designed for residential care in the community, he said we would not need a 'Change of Use' because the planning permission for Mr Warner to change the bungalows into offices had not taken place. Therefore, we would not require a 'Change of Use' as we would be using the bungalow for the same purpose it was originally built for. Praise God for His favour on us.

On Wednesday 13th May, Alison and I met to discuss a few different things. We decided we needed to make an appointment with two banks so we could open two accounts. One for The Healing Rooms and one for The Care Centre. The only problem was we didn't have a name for The Care Centre. We had gathered over thirty possible names, but we hadn't come to a definite decision on one which we both thought was the right one. So, we looked down the list at all the feasible names and asked the Lord to show us which one was the right one. We were getting desperate. We started crossing them off one by one as we both felt they weren't suitable. We then had just four left on our list. I kept reading them over and over to see which one jumped out at me! We finally agreed on The WELL HEAD CENTRE. We both agreed that this was the name God had chosen for us. This name had a good deal of significance:

Firstly – the site next to the bungalow is called The Wellhead Park and The Wellhead Field, so the people of Bourne would know where to find us.

Secondly – Jesus is the head of the well, from which all healing and love flows.

Thirdly – A well head. Meaning your head is now well. Healing for the mind and emotions.

When I prayed and asked the Lord to give us the right name for the Centre, I asked Him to make it clear, to have it on billboards in BIG letters, or even in lights so I wouldn't miss it. In June, it would be Bourne's Annual Festival so all around Bourne posters and signs were advertising this event. On every main road coming into Bourne there was an enormous sign with BIG black letters saying that the Annual Festival would be held on The Wellhead Playing Field, Bourne. Everyone would know where the Well Head Centre is, as they had done our advertising for us! We separated the word Wellhead into two words Well and Head, as we thought it fitted our Centre better. I just knew it was right when I saw these signs. When I came home and told Norman about the name, he got excited about it too. He said, 'Yes, that's it.' God is so good.

One Sunday in the middle of May there was a word of knowledge for someone who kept getting cramps in the legs, so I went forward for that, as I had been getting severe pain in my lower leg for several weeks now. Whilst I was being prayed for, the lady said to me, 'The Lord says don't worry, Janice, everything will be alright. He has put His hedge of protection around you and the pains you have been experiencing will come to nothing.' I was so encouraged by God's goodness to me. He was showing me every step along the way.

That evening, I went to the Corporate Prayer night at church and I was on the Healing Team. The first lady to come to me was a lady who had mental health problems. I prayed with her, and she told me she was healed. Praise God, I believed that was confirmation from the Lord as to what He would do here in Bourne. Isn't God amazing?

Norman had been off work for a week with severe pain in his hip. He worked full time as a Human Resources Manager. The doctor said it was a pulled muscle. The Physiotherapist said it was a torn muscle. Either way he was not able to get comfortable and would pace up and down, sit for a bit, lie down on the bed for a bit, then start the cycle all over again. We could either say it was the devil trying to stop us doing what we were doing, or we could say God has allowed it all to happen and it was His perfect timing. Norman focused on reading healing scriptures, and God was downloading truth to him whilst he was on his own and quiet in the bedroom. We both believed God would use the time to His advantage, that Norman would learn a few things. God's Kingdom would come and His will would be done in our lives and in this place.

On Monday 18 May, God began speaking to me through dreams. In the first one, I was riding my bike along a muddy track when I got so stuck in it all that I had to stop and get off. I didn't know which way I could go to get out of it. Whilst I was contemplating what to do next, a young boy came along. I asked him if there was any other route I could take to get out of this mess. He told me that there was mud everywhere, but there were some places where we could pass around the worst areas and make it through. I took his advice and followed after him. He led me out of it safely. I believe God was showing me that we are going through some challenges, but there was a way through, and if we asked Him and followed His leading, we would make it.

In the second dream, I was driving my car down a fast busy road when the rider of a motor bike in front of me turned round to indicate to me that there was something about to hit me. I saw what looked like a big boulder coming towards me. I couldn't get out of its way, so it came thundering through my windscreen and lodged itself into the left side of my head, neck and shoulders. I panicked and then kept pressing my headlights on and off to attract someone's attention whilst pulling to the side of the road. Once I had stopped, some people came over to me and helped me out of the car and phoned for help. I believe God was showing me that I needed to be ready and prepared and to know that everything would turn out right because He is with me, and no weapon formed against me shall prosper.

Shortly after these dreams, the Salvation Army Officer in Bourne contacted me to tell me he would be happy to be one of our advisors for The Healing Rooms. Then on the last Friday of May, I received written confirmation from SKDC telling us that we DID NOT need planning permission or a 'Change of Use' for the bungalow. This was such good news as we could now begin the process of getting the bungalow ready for use!

At the beginning of June, I received our very first financial provision for The Well Head Centre – a donation of £50 to put into our account. It was like the first fruits of God's promises to us.

Two days after our first financial blessing, Amanda woke me up early in the morning with a phone call to tell me something significant with regards to The Well Head Centre. In a nut-shell, she said that her uncle told her that her mother worked as a psychiatric nurse in a place called 'Well Head House' in Yorkshire, and that is where she was conceived. Amanda was then delivered in Thorpe Hall, Peterborough, which is where Amanda works now as a nurse.

On the 10th June, Alison and I went Prayer walking all around the outskirts of Bourne today. It took us two hours. We were armed with scriptures to read out along the way, and we put little red stickers on trees, lamp posts and street signs as we walked along. The red stickers represented the blood of Jesus. We applied the blood of Jesus everywhere we went. On the final stretch back home, we were singing praise and worship songs at the top of our voices. There were lots of cars going past so no-one heard us! There were specific scriptures we felt we had to read out aloud along the way and they were Psalm 107, John 17:6-25, Joshua 6:1-16 and Joshua 1:5-9. This was the first of seven prayer walks that we felt we should do over the course of the following weeks, some of which included walking in the wind and the rain. We were determined that the weather would not prevent us from pressing into what God was calling us to do.

Two days after our first prayer walk, God brought to my attention Acts 4:8-33. It is all about unity in the churches, so I passed it straight on to Alison and then encouraged her to contact those ministers in the town who had not yet responded to previous emails and letters. We needed as many of the church leaders in the town to partner with us in The Healing Rooms at this time, and we knew that their churches would benefit too.

The following Monday, Alison, Amanda, Norman and myself met to discuss where we would go from here, and what were the next steps we needed to take. When I went to let them in my front door, I noticed on the front lawn loads of white and grey feathers. We assumed a cat had had a run-in with a pigeon. Amanda thought it was a prophetic sign that God is with us. We are under His wings and He is our protection. Norman gave us a feather each! We put forward names of people who could be approached as Trustees for The Well Head Centre, so we could proceed with becoming a charity. God also encouraged us with a scripture tonight, The Prayer of Jabez . . . .

On Thursday later that week, Amanda told me that when she went outside her house there were lots of feathers on her lawn too.

She believed it was a sign of our heavenly Father's double blessing, protection and favour on us. That same evening, we went to the Ely Healing Rooms as part of our training as Directors. It was good to visit other Healing Rooms just to see how it works in different areas. We had a great time of fellowship with the team there and we picked up some ideas for ourselves. Importantly, how to do some things, and how not to do some things! They were very hospitable to us, and we enjoyed the evening with them. They met in a building opposite the Cathedral as they didn't have their own building as we do. We have learned since, that we are the only Healing Rooms in England and Wales with our own building! We picked up some of their literature for us to have a look at to help us when we open up our Healing Rooms. We were blessed as we shared with them.

Soon after, Alison and I went to chat with the vicar at the Church of England Church here in Bourne. We had a great chat with him, and he committed to be one of the Advisors for The Healing Rooms. What an answer to prayer.

Alison's daughter said she would like to take on our quad area at The Well Head Centre. She was at the Grammar School in Bourne and wanted to make it her Year 11 project. It was an overgrown, medium sized garden in the centre of the complex, and Catherine wanted to make it into a prayer and sensory garden for the guests who stay with us. We were thrilled, and couldn't wait to see her plans.

At the end of June, a lady phoned Alison up from a town near Bourne called Stamford. She had been looking at the National Association of Healing Rooms website and had seen our name listed as 'To be opened soon'. She informed us that we were now official and were known all around Great Britain and the world perhaps! It was incredible. Anyway, it seemed that this lady was a preacher in Stamford, Lincolnshire. She was just about to start a three-month sabbatical, and she felt God urging her to get involved in a healing ministry, which is why she was looking at our website. Apparently, she was on the phone to Alison for over an hour! She was so excited when she heard what was planned here in Bourne. We were excited that she had found us on the brand-new website! Praise God. Around this time, God led me to John 27:17 to remind me why He had chosen me for this project. 'Feed my sheep, feed my lambs, take care of my sheep.' Alison told me that she had been given the same scripture, which was a confirmation of our awesome call. I was also encouraged by the fact that we now had sixty people on our Prayer Support Team.

I went to our local painters and decorators in the town today to see if they would like to support us by donating various resources to us to help decorate the rooms.

Shortly after we held another prayer walk in the middle of July, one of our close friends asked me if we needed a washing machine, a fridge freezer, a cooker, bedding and cutlery for the Centre. I was totally amazed and said 'Yes'. He said he would store them all for us until we need them. God was providing everything we needed.

On the 31st July, I received a very large box of decorating materials from one of our local DIY shops. They delivered a box of delights to my door, which included, paint, brushes, filler, tape, rollers, white spirit, trays etc. Everything we needed to get started. I bought some emulsion and some wood preserve so that we could get started the following day. I picked up some boxes from Sainsbury's to put all the broken glass in plus other horrible things which are lying in many of the rooms in the bungalow. My hygienist friend from the local dental practice offered us loads of cleaning materials, including a wallpaper stripper, and told me that she would like to make some of the curtains in the bungalow. Her husband Mark being a tiler, plasterer and electrician, she offered his services too. Here was another specific answer to prayer. As I sent out our monthly Prayer Pointers by email earlier that day. One of the prayer requests was for God to provide us with professional skilled volunteers, such as carpenters, electricians and plumbers. I don't think the ink on the email was even dry yet! WOW.

The next day, we went to the bungalow to start cleaning. When we used the key to try and open the front door lock, it just kept spinning round and getting nowhere. We saw there was also a padlock on the door, but of course, we had no key for that! There were also screws in the door to stop any unwanted intruders getting in. I decided I needed to make a phone call to Warner's. The guy passed the information on to someone else and within about ten minutes a man came round with a hacksaw and cut the padlock off!

Once we were in, we realised we had no electricity or running water which would make it difficult to use the hoover or do any cleaning. While he was still with us, I asked him if he could help us with this small matter. He got onto it straight away, and within an hour we had cold running water and most of the electric sockets were working. We had to let the water run a while as the colour of it was disgusting to say the least. This place had been closed and boarded up for at least six years, so you can imagine! There were leaks in some of the rooms too. One of the rooms in The Healing Rooms end of the bungalow had had youths in there and there had been a fire. All the walls and ceiling were black and sticky. There were nappies, needles, broken glass and other disgusting items on the floor in that room. All in all, we got around all of the twenty-three rooms. We swept up and cleaned all the windows (once we got the boards off!)

We measured up for six replacement windowpanes. We put some wood preservative on the front door frame, so it would look nice for people when they come to the bungalow. Gill (from the dentist) came and measured up for all the curtains, and some ladies cleaned up the kitchen. Whilst we were having some light refreshment in the dining room, our daughter Hazel and her two boys were in there with us and she turned to me and said 'It smells of urine in here, Mum.'

I said, 'Well we are going to shampoo all the carpets so it will be alright, and in any case we haven't any money to replace the carpet so it will have to do for now.'

She replied, 'You can't have this carpet down. It will still smell, I'll replace it for you.' I took her up on her very kind and generous offer.

The most amazing thing happened when a maintenance man from Warners came to help us out. He was the first person to enter the bungalow and he started to ask questions about what we were going to do in there. When I told him about The Well Head Centre and the short-term residential part of it, his eyes welled up and he said to us, 'I've been there.' He then went on to tell us that he went to his GP, who referred him to a hypnotherapist. Apparently she did him some good, but I said, 'That is why we are opening up this place so people don't have to go to a hypnotherapist.' When I walked away, I had to stop myself from crying. I went outside to the car and thanked and praised God for He is so wonderful. He was confirming our plans with signs all the way. The Lord would do some amazing things in this place.

Resources for the Well Head Centre were trickling in. I was offered four small tables, a three-piece suite, a bath and panel for our bathroom when it is ready, twenty-two plastic chairs, a pool table, a computer and some crockery. God is so good.

A Kingfisher

On Wednesday 19 August I went for a trip on the River Taxi in Spalding, just to enjoy the sunshine and to spend some time hearing from God. When I got off the boat at Springfields Shopping Outlet, I met an old friend of mine from Bourne who was waiting to get on the boat. I stopped and chatted to her about various things. Then she told me that she had been depressed because she wasn't working now, and she had just had an operation on her foot to remove a bunion. She had been at home for three months and was very lonely as she hadn't been able to get out and no-one came to visit her. She also told me about her daughter who was depressed and had been referred to a counsellor who made her feel even worse. I already knew about her daughter. I then told her what I was embarking on and asked her if she wanted to help. I told her she could just drop in anytime and have a look around the place.

It was not just some chance meeting. I believed it was a divine appointment and that something good would come out of our meeting together. During my visit to Spalding, I said to God, 'If nothing else happens today, I believe that was a divine appointment and I am happy.' God had other ideas!

Whilst on the boat coming over, I had asked God if I could see dragonflies, as I have before. Well, I saw dragonflies, butterflies and bullfinches. Then on the way back I saw a kingfisher, which I have never seen before. In the car coming home I then saw a heron. God was so good to me. He gave me such a wonderful day with Him. He always gives us so much more than we ask of Him. We just need to look and see what He wants to show us.

The following day, Alison, Amanda and I had a meeting with Philip Warner regarding the lease for the bungalow. There were some slight alterations needed to it, which we discussed and Philip would send it back to his solicitor and have it amended. As soon as it was done the documents could be signed, it would all be official and we could go and inhabit the land!!

He told us that the electricians were in the bungalow making everything safe for us. He was also having the central heating boiler serviced so that it would be working when we needed it. He said he was also sorting out the water and the security on the doors for us. He then said, 'That is it, I draw a line here,' as if to say from now on it's all up to you. We thought we might have to pay towards some of those bills, but he said he would pay for them. So, we came away feeling elated. Philip did say that his solicitor kept on at him for letting us use the bungalow free of charge and that he was paying for things that we should be paying for. But Philip stuck to his guns and did what he thought best. What a blessing he was.

Amanda had been given a picture of a Kingfisher the other day. She said it was significant. It is a KING FISHER, meaning a fisher for the King. A shiver went down me, and I told her about my sighting of the Kingfisher in Spalding. We were all on the same wave-length. The Spirit was opening the eyes of our understanding.

A few days later, Amanda gave me an encouraging word. She told us that God had revealed to her that The Well Head Centre would be operating in San Francisco, USA. We would be taking this ministry over there. When I got home, I looked up a prophecy given to me and Norman in April 2008. It clearly stated that we would be going over to America to minister. We looked forward to all this coming into being.

On the last Thursday in August, I received the Lease Agreement in the post, but it seemed all a bit too complicated for me, so I put it to one side until Norman came home! I sort of got the gist of it. It said that we had to get a solicitor to witness our signatures, so I let Norman read and explain it to me. A few days later I passed the Lease Agreement over to Alison to read.

Whilst we were visiting Grapevine Festival that summer, I took the opportunity to ask a friend of ours, Anton, if he thought Godfrey Birtill (a worship leader at New Life, Lincoln) would be willing to come along to do a Thanksgiving, Dedication and Celebration Service/Praise Party for us when we opened up the Healing Rooms and The Well

Head Centre. Anton attended the same church as Godfrey and knew him very well. He said he thought he probably would come, but he was very busy and very expensive. I was not put off by this and asked him if he would approach Godfrey for us just to see what his reaction would be. In early September, I received an email from Anton, and he said that Godfrey would come! He had given Anton some dates that he had free in his diary and best of all he wouldn't charge! I was so pleased to hear this good news and got on to Alison and Amanda straight away to see which dates were the most suitable for them. God is so good. I thought we could have a 'love offering' for Godfrey, and I'm sure that would more than cover his costs for the evening.

On Sunday 6 September, I took the Lease Agreement into church, and I sat down with a solicitor friend of ours and went through it. I had to repeat on oath what he was saying to me and then I signed the declaration. Then he watched me sign the Lease and witnessed my signature with his. I had now done my part and would pass it on to Alison for her to do hers.

A few days later, Alison went to see a local solicitor and got her part of the Lease Agreement and declaration signed. She then photocopied the relevant bits for me and then sent it back to the solicitors.

Philip Warner then asked me when we wanted to go into the bungalow. Things were moving along nicely.

We compiled a letter to our Prayer Support Team asking them if they would prayerfully consider partnering with us financially in this project. Whilst I was telling Norman about the letter that same evening, I realised that our church was also preparing to launch a Giving Campaign on 4 October. Given that some of our Prayer Support Team are from our church we decided to hold back sending the letters until we had spoken to one of our church leaders.

On Thursday 10 September, I phoned Simon, one of our church leaders about the letters, and he suggested I could just send out the letters to those who were not members of KingsGate Church. I thought that was a good idea. Simon thanked me for letting him know what we were about to do. I spent all morning sending out individual emails to all those who do not attend KingsGate.

On Monday 14 September, Alison and I went to the bungalow together so we could write down everything needing to be done in each room at the Centre. A couple of friends came and prayed with us and prophesied over the bungalow. They said there would be an abundance of fruit, a sweet scent of honey as the people walked into the bungalow. Fresh bread daily would be available. They saw a fridge full of all different varieties of fruit juices. So again, there was an abundance of God's provision. They also felt the three words FAITH, HOPE and TRUST as they walked down the central corridor. They also said that it was going to be a place of life and not death as it was before. Praise God.

Two days later, a group of us met at The Well Head Centre at 1.00pm to pray around the building, anointing the doorposts, planting Bibles at the front and back gardens, and writing scriptures on all the internal walls. When we started off there were seven of us, but many more were praying just where they were. The sun was shining, and we showed around those who hadn't been before. Then we stood in the entrance and started praying. Amanda had a vision of an oil strike. There was oil gushing up and over us, rich, thick oil. She said it was the oil of the anointing showering down on us. We enjoyed just standing in it and accepting all that it represented for The Well Head Centre and us. I also believed it represented abundance of provision for us. Alison, Rosemary and Margaret went and anointed all the rooms with oil and prayed in them. Amanda and I went outside to dig two holes for the Bibles to be planted in the front and back gardens. We planted one at the back door and one at the front. We wanted everything we did in that place to be built on the word of God.

At 6.30pm a couple from KingsGate came over to bring us a bath and bath panel for our bathroom when we got there. I asked a builder friend of ours, Brent, if he thought we could divide the old bathroom into two separate rooms accommodating a bathroom and shower room. He said, 'Absolutely! You have loads of space to do that,' so we would look into putting a stud partition in to separate the two. I then asked him if we could also put an en suite in two of the bedrooms and again he said yes, since space was abundant. So now we just needed a plumber, a builder, a carpenter (to cut a hole in a wall for the new door), an electrician to do all the electrical work and all the fixtures and fittings to go in them! God would provide.

The next day, I phoned Gill (my hygienist) to see if her husband Mark (who is a professional electrician, tiler and plasterer) would be available to do some work for us in the Centre. Whilst talking to her on the phone she told me that she had four pine single beds for us if we wanted them. We just needed to get the mattresses for them. Mark would come over the following afternoon. I would get him to have a look at the room which had a fire in and see if he could sort out some electrics for us.

Gerald was stripping off wallpaper when I arrived at the Centre. The central heating chappie was there trying to sort out the heating and get us some water in the kitchen for us. He was there all day. He had lunch with us and still he was no further solving the mystery. He said the system was obsolete and he didn't have a code number to even get into the system. Later in the day at about 4pm, after he had phoned his boss and told him his predicament, an engineer from Warner's came and had a look in the boiler room and seemed to turn the right wheels and get the water to fill up in the taps in the kitchen. I left them to it as it would probably take ages for the tank to fill up. The heating engineer said there will be another man coming back the following week to try and sort out the heating. The engineer from Warner's would also come to fit the security system on the back door of the bungalow to increase the safety of the place.

During the afternoon, Mark came round to have a look in all the rooms to check all the electrics. Some of the sockets weren't working, so he made a note of all that needed to be replaced. The room which had a fire in it had two new windowpanes put in so was much improved. It was still black from top to bottom, but at least we could see what to do in there. Mark is going to put us two new light fixtures in the ceiling too. There was an old filthy toilet and wash basin in there which will have to be removed. I think it was used as a sluice room in its previous life! It wouldn't really make people feel at ease when they came in for prayer with a messy sink and basin in the room!

During those early days of renovating, I was reading a book called *Could it be Dementia?* by Louise Morse and Roger Hitchings. I had bought it six months previously. I didn't know at the time why I was so drawn to this book. But when I read what was written on page 24, I knew exactly why I had bought it. This is what it said,

'The darkness can speak of miracles, and yes, there are treasures hidden in the darkness.'

And, looking at it through Christian eyes and seeing through the darkness to the treasure hidden there, reminds me of the scripture which we were looking into a few months ago, Isaiah 45:2-3:

'He gives me the treasures of darkness and hidden riches in secret places.'

What a wonder. Everything just falls into its right place when we wait on God.

On Monday 21 September I received an email from Amanda. She said when she woke up after doing the night shift the Lord revealed something to her. We had been to Castle Rising in Norfolk the day before for Sunday lunch and a walk up to the Castle there. We had a wonderful time. The weather was glorious. This is what the Lord revealed to her about our visit.

She saw a Castle, housing a refuge fortress, a strong tower where the enemy cannot enter. There was a flag flying there which means that the King or Queen is in residence.

We believed this indicated that the King is in residence at The Well Head Centre. We would see all classes, high and low, all with sick minds being healed. There is no divide in the purposes of God.

During a subsequent time of family prayer, Norman had a picture of a shute with a ball pool at the bottom of it. He believed God was saying that the people would come to us to be healed, delivered and transformed by the power of God and then go down the shute and end up in a ball pool where there would be things written on these balls for them. Different types of ministries they might walk in, or a new plan and destiny for their lives. They would pick up a ball and know what they should do, or where they would go from then on. They would be totally transformed by God's amazing love. They would come to us in one way and go from us in another. God is in the transforming lives business and He was going to do it. Amen to that.

I went down to the bungalow today as Gerald wanted to go and do some decorating for us, and Keith also wanted to deliver some stuff. Two brand new office desks and a wardrobe to be precise! He said he has got some more things he wants to bring over and he will do that later in the week. Gerald had painted emulsion on the ceiling in the waiting room of the Healing Rooms, put a wood preservative on the window frames and filled all the holes in. He then stripped the 6-inch border off with the help of a steamer! It seemed to be taking ages so I gave him a hand with it, and we both got it off in double quick time. It all looked better already. As we were coming out of the bungalow, a workman from Warner's asked Gerald if we needed a small wheelie bin for us to put all our rubbish in, and so Gerald came to ask me. I said 'Yes, please.' So he went off to fetch us one. Then when he came back with it, he said, 'When it is full, give me a call and I will come and empty it for you, and if you have any paper that needs recycling, let me know and I will recycle that for you too.' So he gave me his mobile number and then left. God's goodness never failed to amaze me.

The following morning Margaret, from Stamford came to deliver some undercoat and gloss paint for us to use in the bungalow. She also put a paint brush and turps in the box. God is so good. He is Jehovah Jireh, our Provider. Keith also brought us a bookcase and a wardrobe.

The next day, Keith phoned me at 8.45am and said he wanted to bring a washing machine to us in forty-five minutes time, so I quickly got ready and went round to the bungalow to meet him. He arrived on time and put the washing machine in the laundry room for me. Then I had a phone call from Mark (my electrician friend) saying that he would be around soon to do some more electrics, so I waited for him to come. Then I went into the laundry room and saw water on the floor. I texted Mick at Warner's and asked him what I should do. He sent someone around to investigate. We found that someone had flushed the sluice bowl and it had flooded over the top because it was blocked with . . . who knows what! He then capped the water off to solve the problem.

Mark did all I needed him to do in the waiting room. Then I waited for Graham (my plumber friend) to come over and have a look at all the basins in the Healing Rooms end of the bungalow. There were basins in all of the rooms which we are going to be using as 'Prayer Rooms' and so we thought it best if we remove them as people who come in for prayer do not want to see basins in the rooms! I hoped he would be able to do the job for us.

At the end of September, Amanda, Norman, Alison, Rosemarie and I went down to Bury St Edmunds to a Healing Rooms Refreshing Day, led by a couple from the USA. On the way down in the car, we were discussing various things about The Healing Rooms and The Well Head Centre. We discussed particularly about our Thanksgiving, Dedication and Celebration Evening that we were planning to have in October in The Centre, thanking God for all his provision for us thus far and all He has promised in the future. Well during the day, one of the teachers spoke about 'The Well is now open,' which was also a word for us from the Director of the Healing Rooms in Ely right at the beginning of the day. Then the guest speaker spoke about an acorn and the oak tree. Later in the day her husband mentioned Godfrey Birtill. We were aghast at all these confirmations for our project all in one day! God is so good.

The next time I went to the bungalow to do some cleaning, I decided to wash down the skirting board in the waiting room ready for the undercoating and do the undercoat as well. Whilst I was there, I just told the Lord I wished someone would come as it was a bit lonely being there all by myself. A few minutes later a man shouted in through the front door. I said, 'Yes, I am in here; come on in.' It was Alan, the waste disposal and recycling guy from Warners. He told me he had just emptied my skip and taken the large black bag full of old wallpaper. He said, 'If I have to come around three times a day to empty it I will. Put what you want in it and I will take it and dispose of it for you.' When I asked him if Philip Warner knew he was doing this for us, he kindly said, 'My boss does and he says it is OK!' He then asked me what we were doing in the bungalow. When I told him, he too had watery eyes and said, 'I bet you get the other bungalows too!' He was so thrilled to be able to help us in such a small way (or so he thought). God is so good.

One day in early October, I had in my mind 'Sugar Soap' for some unknown reason! I remembered it from the days when I worked in an ironmongers shop about twenty years before! I couldn't quite remember what it was for, so on my walkabout around the town, dropping Prayer Pointers off locally to people on our Prayer Support Team, I just popped into Harrison & Dunn's, to ask them for some really strong disinfectant and some 'Sugar Soap.' Sugar soap is used for preparing walls before painting if there has been any mess, such as nicotine, smoke damage or any other substance that needs removing before painting or wallpapering. It was exactly what was needed to clean the smoke damaged room before emulsioning. God definitely knows what we need to get all the jobs done! To top it all, just before I left the bungalow that day, a white dove came down onto the car park where I was loading up my car to go home. I just stood and watched it for a while, amazed at God's awesomeness.

Shortly after the experience with the white dove, I went away for a holiday in the Cotswolds. I finished reading *Could it be Dementia?* by Louise Morse and Roger Hitchings. You know God has a plan for everything, and at church the following weekend, I had a couple who came out for healing prayer at the end of our service. The lady had arthritis and her husband had . . . you've guessed it . . . dementia. I knew there was a reason for me reading that book when I did. The book had said that people with dementia are 'sharing in Christ's sufferings', Philippians 3:10. They feel so sad, lonely and rejected, just like Jesus felt when He went to the cross. We were all crying when I said this to the gentleman. I knew this was not how we are supposed to minister, so I pulled myself together and then prayed for them both. Nothing is ever wasted in God's economy. He can use us if we allow Him to. I was so blessed and humbled that God chose to use me in this way and felt sure it was all preparation for when The Healing Rooms and The Well Head Centre opened. He is changing us from one degree of glory to another, step by step.

I went over to Peterborough to the house of another friend who offered to do our stationery for us. I wanted to get it all sorted out on the computer once and for all so we could get some letters printed off and start contacting businesses and organisations for some financial help. It all went well and she would get them printed and sent to us. The letter heads looked fantastic. I also talked to her about an email address and website for The Well Head Centre. We would have one page on the website with The Well Head Centre 'Mission Statement' on, with a link to The Healing Rooms. Everything seemed to be coming along nicely.

On Saturday 10 October we started our 'Week of Decorating'. It was a hive of activity. We emulsioned the waiting room walls and ran out of the emulsion, so we had to water it down to make it last! We hoped no one would notice! Amanda and I undercoated the radiators in the Dining Room. Gerald and Peter H prepared the windows for when the glass arrives on Monday. Peter also cleared out all the gutters as they were overflowing with moss and other nasty stuff! This would avoid the rain pouring over the top! I cleaned, bleached and disinfected the dining room floor to try and get rid of the smell which had hung around in the carpet previously. Another couple washed all twenty-one radiators in the bungalow to get them ready for painting. Wallpaper was stripped off in one of the Prayer Rooms too. Later in the day, Amanda and I used loads of buckets of sugar soap to try and clean the soot off the walls in one of the prayer rooms.

We had loads of furniture delivered too. A three-piece suite, a dining table and chairs, a long dining room cupboard, two sets of bunk beds and more curtains. Praise God.

On Monday, I received a beautiful card from my most precious sister in Christ, Linda. She wrote such wonderful words in the card to me that I couldn't read it all at once because tears were welling up in my eyes. I believe it was a prophetic card. The words she wrote were straight from God's heart to me. She said He wanted me to know that. The picture on the front was a pair of pink shoes, and the words read, 'There is no-one who can fill these shoes like you can.' Everyone knows I am a shoe person, so that was just me!

Later in the day whilst I was at the bungalow, Amanda phoned and told me that God wanted me not to worry, that everything would fall into its right place. The provision would come, and even if it wasn't all done by 30th when Godfrey is coming, it won't matter. People would come and see what still needed to be done, catch the vision and come on board with us. We had the power that brought creation into being. We had 'El' our powerful Father God on our case. It was God's project, not mine. I was just a co-labourer in His Kingdom purposes.

On Tuesday 13th October, Alison and I did the second group of interviews for the Healing Rooms Ministry Team. All went well, and they all seemed up for it and ready to go. We just had four more people to see and then we could arrange for some practical training sessions for us all. It would be a good time for us to get to know each person on the team and pray for one another.

Over those last few weeks, I was learning how to walk in humility. I felt God wanting to teach me to do that. He was teaching me to walk and live above 'reproach.' I didn't really know what that meant, but it seemed every time I opened up my Bible, that word kept popping out at me. I looked it up in the dictionary and my thesaurus, and it means disgrace, blame, unrighteousness etc. I believed God was refining me even more along my journey with Him. I prayed every day that I would live my life above reproach as it says in His word:

'Just as He chose us in Him before the foundation of the world, that we should be holy and without blame before Him in love.' Ephesians 1:4

I knew that if God was going to use me, He had to change some parts of my character. It was not easy as I fail most days. But I was on a journey, and I knew God would bring to completion that which He had begun. I chose to be a woman of integrity.

The next day, whilst I was at The Well Head Centre, Mary B turned up to help. She was so thrilled to be able to come. She offered to help me get the border off the smoke damaged room (now referred to as 'the fire room!'). We didn't realise it was even there until we started washing the walls down ready for Mark to plasterboard the ceiling.

Whilst Mary and I were in the fire room, we noticed some water on the floor in the corner where there were the remains of some pipes, so I phoned Mick at Warners, and within a few minutes someone was round to fix the problem for us. I told him about the fact that we still had no hot water in the kitchen. I don't know what he did, but we did eventually have water coming out of both taps in the kitchen even though the colour of it was a little suspect! Anyway, he did what he could and then left. It was about 4.00pm when I decided to make my way home. As I was leaving, I saw that the boiler room door was open, so I popped in to see if anyone was around. There was a man from Warners and a man from a heating company too. They were trying to sort out the heating and water system for us. They proposed putting a regulator in our bungalow so we could regulate when the central heating and water would be on, and it would only be for our bungalow and not all the others too. It seemed that the idea was good, but it was going to be too expensive. The heating engineer suggested a simpler way of doing things, and we left it in Mr Warner's hands to decide whether to go for it or not!

Just before I left the site to finally go home, an old friend popped in to see me. She used to work in these bungalows when they were occupied by adults with special needs. She told me that when she heard they were going to be closed down, she and another lady went around all the bungalows and claimed them for God's glory. My heart was stirred by this knowledge.

As I went around the bungalow, I came across a calendar on the back of one of the bedroom doors. It was showing October 2003, which would have been the last month the previous occupants were in the bungalow. That is exactly six years to the month when it closed down. God had it all in His plan then.

That morning as I was having my prayer time, I asked the Lord if He would teach me how to pray like He prayed. Not some strategic, step-by-step, well-rehearsed prayer, but one that would get the job done and be totally unique and personal to that person. I was just considering that every time Jesus prayed, He always prayed for people's healing, and then He said, 'Go and sin no more.' He knew they were in sin, but that didn't stop Him praying for their healing. He met their immediate need. So I said to Him, 'When I pray, I don't want to judge or condemn them, but I would still like to know a bit about them and then after I have prayed for their healing, take things a step further by introducing them to Jesus, by getting them to say the Salvation Prayer, then their lives will truly be changed for the better.' Anyway, I started doing my daily Bible reading which was John 16:12-15, and verses 14 and 15 really spoke to me. Then as I read the Kingdom Dynamics (extra teaching in my Bible) I found the answer to the prayer I had prayed five minutes earlier! It said this...

'Teach the things Jesus taught, in the way He taught them, always staying in tune with the Father. Do the things He did in the manner in which He did them. Jesus treated people with dignity, was motivated by compassion and never did anything to selfishly draw attention to Himself, or to perform based on others' agendas. Work with Jesus to see all nations (groups of people) become His followers.'

WOW, WOW, WOW. That was a lightening answer to my prayer today. He just told me how I was to minister to people, the way Jesus did. It was incredible!

Whilst I was in the bath that evening, I was thanking God for all His goodness to us throughout this project, when I realised that Warners Printers are open 24/7. They have maintenance men, fitters, engineers, plumbers and gas fitters on hand all around the clock. I thought to myself, 'Where is there that we could have chosen to do this project that would be better than where we are right now?' I quickly came to the conclusion that there was nowhere, and as I did, I laughed out loud! God is so good at arranging everything if we give Him the opportunity to do it.

I was reminded that when I called Warners due to the water on the floor in one of the prayer rooms, within minutes there was someone there. When I needed the skip emptying, I just called Alan on his mobile and he came and emptied it for us. We had got it all for FREE. We even had 24-hour protection over the place as there were security cameras all around Warners, which looked out over our bungalow too. I just kept laughing at God's favour on us. More and more I was beginning to realise this. This was God's 24/7 Rapid Response Service, all laid up for us!

On the 15th October, I received the news that The Well Head Centre website had gone live. This was such encouraging news after another busy day renovating and decorating the Centre.

Whilst we were at the centre, Peter had made us some lovely brown bread rolls in his bread maker and brought them in for us to share, along with some sliced turkey and some chutney. Amanda had brought some yogurts and some fruit, so we had a feast. We sat in the large dining room to eat at the table. It no longer smelt of urine in there, so it was fine! The disinfectant, bleach, cleaning materials and the smell of paint had got rid of all other unpleasant smells!

All that week I was thinking about this book I felt stirred to write. I never thought in my wildest dreams that I would consider writing a book that someone would like to read. But as I talked to people about it, it spurred me on to actually go through with it. I had read *Miracle Valley*, and *The Grace Outpouring*, and that helped me to realise how such books can help others who are considering or waiting to do something like this. I know how much those books helped me, so I became determined to see it through. I was talking to Mary this week and she was a great encouragement to me, as she was saying things like, the money we get for the sale of the books will help keep the Centre open. I had never really thought of it like that before. Norman asked me to ask God for a title for this book, so that is what I did.

Amanda, Alison, Rosemary and I planned to go in to the bungalow this morning to pray, seek God and repent for all that went on there before we went in, and to take communion. Actually, Alison didn't make it as one of her daughters was not well. We had a wonderful time together.

We have a happy band of helpers in again today decorating the bungalow. We are getting to know each other better as we meet week by week. We don't get much time at church as we are all busy doing our jobs and serving others. I chatted with a lady called Chris at church today who was very interested in coming to see how The Healing Rooms works. I have invited her to a Training Weekend in November to have a taster. She is going to have a chat with her husband to see if it is OK with him for her to come on that weekend. She told me that she has written a book about her life and experiences and so I am looking forward to reading it. She encouraged me to write one! So here it is.

In the following days, work continued on the bungalow. Mark our electrician came and fitted plasterboard to the fire-damaged ceiling in the fireroom, giving it a brightness it didn't have before. We put a seal on all the previously black walls and replaced all the smashed windows. We also removed the disgusting toilet and sink in the fireroom in readiness for transformative emulsion and carpets. It reminded me of the way God sometimes has to strip our lives of unhealthy thought patterns and sin in order to enable us to be used by Him more effectively.

Alison and I went to speak at a Methodist Council Meeting to give them a presentation about The Healing Rooms. They wanted to hear all about the vision and to know if they could help us financially. They were very welcoming to us and received what we had to say. They asked us if we had a budget to which we 'No', as we hadn't any idea how much the building would cost us to run at that stage. We suggested that they should seek God as to how much they should contribute to The Healing Rooms. We would leave it up to them and God.

When we came out of the meeting, Alison and I were having a chat in the car park. She told me that she was feeling that the whole project was too much for her. She had a vision for The Healing Rooms, but not really for the 24/7 Well Head Centre Project. She told me that she had lots of other commitments which she felt she had to honour, plus family commitments. She didn't want to be Assistant Manager of The Well Head Centre either. She said she was finding it difficult, coping with all the demands made upon her. She said she needed to seek God on this and she would get back to me. I had a feeling that she wasn't enjoying all the commitment to the project. It all seemed too much for her. I need to pray about this too as I really need someone to help and support me in this, as I don't feel that I can cope with this all on my own. When I came home and told Norman what Alison had said, I asked him if he wanted to help me manage the day-to-day running of The Well Head Centre but he too felt he couldn't because he was still working full-time in a stressful, managerial job plus he had leadership responsibility at church. I felt quite alone at that point. Alison had said that she thought Norman and I should do it together, but Norman said that wasn't possible at this moment in time. So now I know I am on my own in this. Or am I? I give it all to God. He tells me, 'Be anxious for nothing, fear not and do not worry' I leave it all with Him.

In the middle of October, I had an interesting email from someone called Russell. No-one seemed to know who he was. He wanted to know about the format of the celebration evening we were planning, and how much it cost to get in. So I emailed him back and asked him where he got this information from. He responded telling me he saw it on Godfrey Birtill's website. I quickly went on to it myself and there it was. On Friday 30 October – Healing Rooms Bourne! I was both amazed and shocked to see that on Godfrey's website. Anyway, I emailed him back and told him all about the evening and asked him where he was from. It was a reminder to me that God was at work in this, bringing circumstances and people together for His Kingdom purposes.

Work on the bungalows was continuing. We had two overhead projectors for the Godfrey Birtill celebration and the place was a hive of activity with our team helping out with painting, cleaning and carpet laying.

Shortly after tea on the 27th October, the phone rang. It was my son-in-law Matt, from Lincoln. His voice sounded strained and panicky. He was anxious about our daughter Hazel who left the house at 6.45am to go to Derby University to do her final exam for CBT (Cognitive Behavioural Psychotherapy). She knew she would have to wait until everyone else had completed their exam paper before she would be told whether or not she had passed. Norman had already told me that he had tried to get through to her at lunch time, but couldn't. Hazel had said she would call us early evening to let us know how she had got on. Getting back to Matt, I could totally understand why he was so distraught. I said, 'Let's pray about this.' I started to pray. I prayed for her safety, her protection and that she would contact us within the next half an hour. When I had finished praying, Matt said, 'Amen, but I am still panicking!' We pondered whom we could contact. Matt had already tried the University, but the switchboard was closed. He thought of trying A&E in Derby or even the police, but just as we were thinking of what to do next, his mobile phone rang. It was his mother, saying that Hazel was at her house. I said, 'Why is she there?' and Matt said, 'Because we had planned to go there later this evening!' Matt was so pleased to get that call. I said, 'Matt, that's an answer to prayer.' Whilst we were still on the phone, God answered our prayer!

At 8.45pm, after I had washed up and done the ironing, I decided to give Hazel a call just to see if everything was OK. She told me she had texted Dad (Norman) and Glyn (our son) and so assumed that I had heard that she had passed her final exam. Little did she know that they were at the Centre and I was at home! Anyway, it was a long story, with a catalogue of errors, plus lots of traffic. She was a little frazzled too, but we were so pleased that all was well.

When Norman came home at 9.30pm, I went over all the events of the evening. Apparently, he and Glyn both had texts from Hazel so she had assumed I knew as she thought we were at home together, so she was sorry that she hadn't contacted me too. The gang got loads done in the bungalows, but we would still not have everything finished for when Godfrey comes to help us celebrate how good our God is for getting us this place. We resigned ourselves to that fact, trusting that it would still be an awesome evening.

When I arrived at the Centre the following day, I noticed all the hedges and shrubs had been cut back. They looked amazing. It seemed someone from Warners had been round in the morning and pruned them for us. God is so good. We had another delivery of goods. Peter brought us some glasses, plates, blankets, towels and some other kitchen stuff. Our storeroom was bulging at the seams!

Margaret, Amanda and I did some cleaning and tidying up to get the Centre ready for Friday evening. The carpets were all steamed at least once. The carpet in the corridor where there was a fire, was still more black than pink, but we would have to make do for now. In the meantime, Norman painted the entrance and toilet walls and didn't arrive home until 9.30pm.

Friday 30 October. A special day for us. I couldn't get to my emails fast enough that morning. I really needed to hear from Godfrey about the evening. After quickly scanning my emails, I was so relieved to see that he had contacted me. Apparently, he hadn't received the programme I had sent to him on an attachment, so I sent it again. He had only one set of acetates, so I said if he came early enough, we could perhaps go to the stationers down in the town and get some more done. I went off down to the Centre and washed and tidied up the toilet, as Norman had left a mess after his painting work! I had to sweep up some glass, as he had dropped a frame from off the wall and it had smashed. I washed the kitchen floor, and then Amanda and Gerald came and brought some beautiful lilies and arranged them in three of the rooms. Then they went around cleaning the windows. Everything sparkled.

When I phoned Godfrey to see what time he was arriving he didn't pick up my call. He called me back to say he was caught in traffic and Norman told him a different way to come to try and avoid the worst of it. He told us that he had sent me another email with all the words for the songs on, so we could just print them off and then put them straight on to acetate. It was getting quite late by now, and to make things worse our printer wasn't working either. I quickly forwarded the email to Alison and asked her if she could print them off for us. She said she had some acetates so would print the words straight onto them. We all got ready and went to the Centre at about 5.45pm. There was such a buzz around the place. We all got stuck in, doing what needed to be done, sorting out the drinks and food and so on. Alison made a fruit punch, (she is good at that!) plus some nibbles. Other people brought food too. It was a wonderful spread.

Godfrey arrived at about 6pm and got straight into setting his gear up in the lounge. We were using the lounge, the dining room and the corridor in-between! We had no heating and nothing on the floor in the dining room, but we made the place as welcoming as we could. Norman was outside taking care of things in the car park. Our car park is only big enough for about twelve cars so we limited that to those with blue badges. We knew there would be more than that coming tonight. Warners had given us permission to use their car park over the road from our bungalow, which was handy. Malcolm was across the road showing people the way into Warner's car park. Everyone started pouring in. We gave them a tour round the bungalow and then offered them some food and drink. There were people everywhere! It was a great atmosphere to have so many people in the place at last.

At 7.30pm we were ready to start the evening of Celebration, Dedication and Thanksgiving. Godfrey wanted to sing a more traditional song to begin with to get everyone together so we did that first. I then welcomed everyone including Godfrey, and thanked them all for coming. I said a little about how it all came into being and then read some verses from Isaiah 60 and 61. Afterwards I passed over to Godfrey and he sang the song which Amanda played to me on our way to speak to Mr Warner the first time. It was called 'Fertile Ground'. We had asked Godfrey to sing that song as it meant so much to us. It included the words 'no longer desolate, this is fertile ground where children of the promise are found!' Norman then led us all in prayers of thanksgiving for all those who had helped and supported us over the last 11 months. Godfrey then sang two more of his songs. Amanda then led us in prayers of dedication. Godfrey then sang two more songs and then we went into celebration mode. Whilst we were celebrating there were chocolates being thrown around ('Celebrations' of course!).

During the evening we had a Love Offering for Godfrey as he didn't charge us for coming. Alison rounded off the evening with thanks and comments about the Healing Rooms and The Well Head Centre, and then Godfrey closed the evening with 'Fertile Ground' again. I then spoke a blessing over everyone. It had been an incredible night. Everyone that came were totally blown away by it all. Lots of people caught the vision. Many had not realised the enormity of the project and were re-ignited, encouraged and up for it now more than ever. We were given some prophetic words and pictures as well as some encouraging scripture verses so we were encouraged too. At 9.45pm we all went home.

At church that Sunday, I met quite a few people who had attended our Celebration, Dedication and Thanksgiving evening on Friday night. They were all very excited about the vision. Someone gave me an envelope with the explanation of a picture she had on Friday evening whilst she was there. It was amazing. Also, a lady told me that a friend who she brought with her was suffering from depression when she came in, and it was lifted before she went home! We prayed beforehand that people would be healed during the evening, and God answered our prayer. Another person said he thought that God was revealing to him as he was worshipping, that one of Mr Warner's family members would come and ask for healing and they would be healed. Acts 28:7–10 was the scripture he had to confirm this.

Another lady approached me to have a five-minute chat about something that had happened to her thirty years ago. She was the eldest of three children. Her mother was suffering from depression as she was going through the menopause. The doctors referred her to a mental health hospital in Rauceby, Lincolnshire. She had to take her mother there as she, being the eldest, had signed the consent form for her mother to go for a one-month stay. She went on her own, and she passed through Bourne to get there. On the way back, her car broke down. She was outside the Police Station in Bourne so she went in to get help. Having received the help she needed she went back home safely. When she came to our Celebration Evening on Friday evening, all those memories came flooding back. She believed that if there was a place then like we were opening now, she would have brought her mother here. Previously the bungalows were closed and boarded up. They used to contain the clients but when we open, they would be healed, delivered and set free by the power of God's love. They would return to their own environments and be able to cope with life so much more than before. This is what we believed God was calling us to do. We would be doing exactly the opposite to what had been done before in this place. The enemy was not amused, but we didn't care! I prayed for her as I could see all those memories were bringing back the pain she went through at that time. She was so pleased that we had been obedient to God's call on our lives and it would make a difference to people's lives here in Bourne and beyond.

By this time, we had over one hundred names on our prayer partner's list. I sent out letters to all our prayer partners at KingsGate Community Church asking them if they would like to partner with us financially, and sent out November prayer pointers to all our existing prayer partners.

Around this time, we became 'open-plan' to Warners as the fence between us blew down in the strong winds and all the fence panels were stacked up in our car park! We waited to see what they would do about that. It was quite exciting. Every time we went to the bungalow things had changed! It was all done for us and we didn't have to even pay for it. God is so good. We also managed to get gas and electricity registered for the property so we would be able to keep the place warm at last. God was continuing to bless us with unexpected provision too, of furniture, equipment and finances.

On Thursday 12 November, we held our first Advisory Board Meeting for The Healing Rooms. There were representatives from the Baptist Church, the Methodists, the Church of England and KingsGate Community Church. The Salvation Army Major couldn't make it as he had got Swine Flu. We had a great time chatting together and getting to know each other and discussing how we could move forward from here. There was total unity in the meeting and Alison and I felt a strong sense of support and encouragement from them all.

The following day, I received an email from our church leadership asking me to give them a breakdown of all expenses which we thought we would incur in the setting up of The Well Head Centre. Suddenly, this seemed a bit scary to me, as we should have to sit down and discuss all that was entailed.

That weekend, Matt, Haze and the boys (our daughter, son-in-law and their two boys Zach and Ben) came over so that Matt could make an early start on the laminate flooring in the dining room. Well, he started at about 4pm with the expert help of one of his friends. We were impressed that they were nearly all done by 6pm! It looked great, and it smelt a lot better too!

That Sunday, I spent some time praying with Amanda before the second service at our church. Whilst I was praying, the Lord gave Amanda a picture of two golden vessels, (chalices she called them) which were being filled to overflowing with the blood of Jesus. This blood flowed out and down the side of the golden vessels and onto the floor. Amanda said that we were carriers of His glory and that everywhere we went we would carry His glory and that people's lives would be transformed. We were filled with His glory and fire.

The next Monday, Alison and I went to speak at the Mothers' Union Meeting in a little village near Bourne called Thurlby. We were well received by the ladies. They were genuinely interested in what was about to happen here in Bourne. We invited them to come along when we had our 'Open Day' on Saturday 28 November. Some said they would love to come.

On Thursday 19 November, Norman and I went over to Stamford to visit Homebase so we could get some paint for the Centre. Whilst I was there a 'spirit of boldness' came upon me! I asked the Manager if she had any tins of paint that were dented, or pots of paint that people had mixed together and then not liked the colour and wanted to get rid of them? She asked someone out the back to check and see if there were any and they brought out a large crate of old tins of paint. They were dented tins, old tins and unwanted tins of paint. She said they would all be thrown on the skip so I could take as much as I needed. We had a good look at them all and came away with about ten tins of emulsion. They didn't ask for any identification from us, but just seemed to trust that we were who we said we were. We must have looked a trustworthy pair!! God is so good. He always goes ahead of us. All we have to do is step out and ask.

The following Monday, I had an appointment with Mick from Warners to talk about a few things such as heating, lights, hot water etc. He told me that an engineer would be fitting a part on the heating system on Wednesday which would cost them £400. This would enable us to be isolated from the other three bungalows. I also told him that some of the exterior lights weren't working and so he said he would look into it for us.

Norman and I returned in the evening to do some more emulsioning in the lounge. It was coming on a treat. Norman said he felt the Lord had just spoken to him and said that we are called to be missionaries in our own country. This was such an encouragement, especially given that I was feeling a little low. It felt that progress was happening at a very slow pace. All my volunteers seemed to have vanished into thin air! There was so much to do and I was somewhat overwhelmed by it all.

We were planning 'practise sessions' for The Healing Rooms team over the next three weeks to be ready for 7 January 2010 when we opened to the public. We also had an Open Day planned for Saturday 28 November from 10am–4pm and we still had so much to do to get the bungalow ship-shape for then including getting our website in place. A young man who Alison knew from the Baptist Church in Bourne had offered to do the website for us so Alison and I spent some time planning what we wanted to be on the website.

On the Thursday before the Open Day, I went to a 'People of Influence' lunch at KingsGate. It was very informative and encouraging. We had a lovely lunch and a DVD to watch. Then we had an assessment chart to fill in. Whilst I was there, I was sat on a large table with about seven others. I started talking to one of our stewards from church. He hadn't heard about The Healing Rooms or The Well Head Centre, so I told him as much as I could before the teaching started. When I had finished explaining all about our project, he told me he came to Bourne on a regular basis to do people's gardens and was willing to come and have a look at our property to see if he could help us in any way with ours. He didn't realise how big our property was at that time! He was the owner of a very successful landscape gardening business so I was chuffed that he wanted to come and help us. He also wanted to be added to our Prayer Support Team too, bless him. All in all, it was quite an interesting lunch. I love those sort of days that God arranges for me. It didn't finish there though. Whilst I was at the lunch I was covered in gold dust again, all on my hands and legs. God is so amazing.

For our training sessions at The Healing Rooms we had asked people we knew if they wanted to come and be guinea pigs as it was our first session. We eagerly awaited to see who turned up. I read Isaiah 45:2-3 again. It kept me fired up, knowing that God is in total control and I need not be anxious for anything.

> *'I will go before you and make the crooked places straight. I will break in pieces the gates of bronze and cut the bars of iron. I will give you the treasures of darkness and hidden riches of secret places, that you may know that I, the Lord, Who call you by your name, Am the God of Israel.'*

Everything went really well at our first practise session. No-one came in for prayer so we prayed for three of the team. We did it in the same way it would be done on a normal Healing Rooms evening. We brought in four heaters to put in the four rooms that were being used so we weren't cold. We had our 'Waiting Room' where people sat on comfy sofas waiting to be called in for ministry. Then we had two rooms with teams of three ready to minister and another room set aside for our team of intercessors. We started with worship then we broke bread together and prayed. We then sorted out who was going to be in which team. The intercessors went off into their room and started to pray for all which would take place that evening and to pray for all those coming in for prayer. I was on reception and whilst I was waiting for people to arrive, I had my Bible open at Zechariah chapter 4. This was not normally something that happens to me but I believed

God wanted to say something to me that evening. I read verses 1 to 4 and it was all about Zerubbabel. Reading from verse 6 it says:

> *'This is the word of the* LORD *to Zerubbabel. Not by might, nor by power, but by My Spirit, says the* LORD *of Hosts.'*

Verse 9 reads:

> *'The hands of Zerubbabel have laid the foundations of this temple, His hands shall also finish it then you will know that the* LORD *of Hosts has sent Me to you.'*

The 'Kingdom Dynamics and Word Wealth' sections in my Bible that accompany this portion of scripture are insightful. This is part of what it says:

> *'In the present reference, God informs the re-builder of the temple that the task would not be accomplished through the force of an army, nor through the muscular power or physical stamina of the workmen. Rather, it would be accomplished by the empowering of the Spirit of God.'*

It goes on to say,

> *'The greatest displays of God's power are not necessarily shows of force, mighty acts, or creative splendour. Rather, the supremacy of God's power is seen in the ways He accomplishes His purposes through mere vessels of clay made mighty because He has enthused them with His life. This text addresses a worn-out Zerubbabel, who, having gallantly laid the temple's foundation was about to succumb to discouragement. But the word of God makes a declaration that, by the Spirit of God, Zerubbabel's hands will complete the work God has destined for him. As long as the heart is turned toward Him in childlike trust, He will enable anyone to complete the work to which He has called them.'*

I really needed to hear those words; it was such an encouragement to me.

Saturday 28 November, was our Open Day. The morning started off really well. We had quite a few visitors enjoying the experience. It all went quiet in the afternoon with only six people visiting us. All those who came were fully on board with our vision, and could see it all coming into fruition. We had 'Standing Order Mandates' on the table in the entrance and we prayed that some would take one home with them and consider partnering with us financially.

Norman did a few odd jobs in the Centre whilst it was quiet. He put up three blinds in The Healing Rooms end and a curtain rail in the toilet. Amanda and I ironed three pairs of curtains and put them up in the Waiting Room and toilet. It was all coming together as I imagined. Mark (our electrician/plasterer) came for most of the day to plaster the fireroom ceiling. It looked so much brighter than it did before! He also checked some of the electrics in The Well Head Centre and found a small problem that he would have to investigate at a later date.

On the first Tuesday in December, we had our second practise session for The Healing Rooms. We had a great time ministering to two more members of the team. There were only six of us there but we believed there would be many more, and many more lives would be touched and transformed. We had two in the intercessors room, one on reception and three in the prayer room. Whilst we were worshipping, Jo had a picture of an oak tree and then an acorn. She felt God was saying that like an oak tree starts as an acorn and grows into a large oak tree, though we are small in number today, we shall grow big like an oak tree.

I don't think Jo knew the significance of her picture so we would have to tell her. Jo also told me that her husband was a good tiler and he offered to do any tiling that we needed doing. I planned to ask him to help tile the bathroom and shower room.

The next day, one of the pastors from our church came over to have a look around the Centre. She was thrilled to see it in its present state. She prayed with me in the Waiting Room and she said she saw doves all around the place. The peace of God was there to heal and restore broken lives.

Alison and I went to the Thurlby Methodist Council Meeting to talk to them about The Healing Rooms. We had a great time and they seemed to take in all that we said. We would now wait to see if they were willing to partner with us.

One morning early in December, I had a phone call from a friend who said she had been praying for me most of the night. She said she saw rays of fire coming upon me and flowing through me to touch other people's lives. She also said she felt God was saying to me that I have done all I can do, now I must stand back and watch what only He can do. I really needed to hear that.

That same day, we had our third practise session for The Healing Rooms. Jo had another picture for us during worship. Her picture was of us all at the start of a race, and she felt God was saying to us 'Get ready, be prepared.' Also, another member of the team had a picture for us from the Lord:

'I saw a ring of light – it was yellow in colour and suspended in the darkness. Each member of the Healing Rooms team was as a shining star, a diadem through which the ray passed. I believe that the ring should be seen as a crown. Majestic! A power none can contend. Be still my human spirit and know that I am God. I have provided the way, a new and living way. My way is truth, righteousness, peace, justice, but above all love. I have provided you a ring of light that binds you all together. Step into the light which shines brightest in the darkest places.'

Also, during our prayer time one of the team said out loud these words from the Lord:

'You have done all you can, now watch what I will do.'

I believe that word was for me, to confirm the word which I had heard earlier. God is so good. He knows exactly what we need and when we need it.

We were still waiting for the heating and water to be sorted out and so had to keep moving our freestanding heaters around from one room to another. We thanked God that it was such a mild December and the sun shone through the windows so we felt warm! We saw a Muntjac deer walk across our garden whilst worshipping. It must have come from the nearby woods. He seemed to be enjoying his freedom in our grounds! We stood and watched him for a while. He seemed quite content. We believe it was a prophetic picture for the people who will be coming into The Well Head Centre that they will feel safe, secure and content in this place and will also experience their freedom. It was truly amazing. We had seen doves, squirrels, a cat, a dog, some ducks and now a deer.

The following day, I received an email from Mr Warner with regards the Council Tax. Apparently, Warners had already paid the £2200 for the year, so they would send me a bill for the length of time we have been in the bungalow. That will be from September to January. This would cost us around £1000. I took a sharp intake of breath, switched my computer off and came downstairs. I said to myself, 'How do we pay a bill for £1000 when we only have £850 in our bank account? Well God knows and He will sort it.'

I was eagerly waiting to hear from three different sources whom I have written to ask for financial support for our project.

On Thursday 10th December, we had our final practise session. It went really well. We prayed for two more of our team and one lady from the Baptist Church in Bourne. By this point, we had prayed for all the team so we were all prayed up and ready to go, and would take a short break over the Christmas period.

Norman said it might be a good idea to phone SKDC to see if we needed to pay this £1000 or whether we were entitled to some discount. So, I did phone them and they were very helpful. They would send someone out to have a look at the bungalow to see what they can do for us.

Shortly afterwards, I had a phone call from Mark (our electrician) to say he would be free that afternoon at around 3.30pm if I was around. He wanted to put some lights up in the fire room. So, I arranged to meet him there. When he had done them, he phoned me to say, 'You may need sunglasses when you go in there!' This may mean that we only need one ceiling light rather than the two we had been planning, although it might all look different once we get the walls painted and the curtains up.

On Tuesday 15 December, I received a text from our builder friend with a quote for some work we needed doing on the bathroom and to create two en suites. His quote was £5,000 plus VAT. For the bathroom alone it would cost around £2,000. I took a sharp intake of breath and thanked him for that information. It included everything except painting and decorating. We would put it into our budget and see what happened!

I had been trying to get hold of the person in charge of a similar organisation in Lincoln. This place was called The Haven and accommodated up to five vulnerable people. There were fully qualified staff in this house as well as professionals coming in to give help and therapy but the set-up is the same. I thought it would be helpful for us to go over and see if they could help us in any way. Shortly before Christmas, I had a phone call from The Haven and so we arranged to go over on 6th January 2010 to have a look at their work.

I was feeling a bit wobbly. Sometimes I would wake up and think, 'How on earth am I going to get all the things I need for this project and where's the money, expertise and manpower going to come from?' Then I realised, it wouldn't be me who did any of it. I needed to pass it all over to my Heavenly Father who would do it ALL. I had to keep reminding myself what a small part God wanted me to play in all of this. He would do the greater part. Hallelujah!

We had a Directors Meeting to discuss the budget for the year and the set-up costs so we could present some figures to those organisations that require it. Once this was completed, we were able to send it to all interested parties.

We realised that our mail was not getting through as people had sent us items which had not arrived. I needed to go to the post office to investigate! On the last Wednesday before Christmas, I had a chat with the postman who told me that all mail to 12 Manor Lane (our bungalow), had been re-directed to Peterborough and they would return it to the sender, but only if there was an address inside! I decided to check it all out and so I sent a card to 12 Manor Lane and it never arrived. Hopefully now things will filter through and we will start to receive all our mail.

We are still believing for cheques in the post, gifts and surprises, so I'm sure we will start to get some!

Shortly after Christmas, we had visitors come over from our church in Peterborough. They had been wanting to come and see the bungalow for some time. We showed them around and the first thing I noticed was a brand-new wooden fence all around the car park and alongside the driveway. The previous fence had blown over with very strong winds and we were open to the elements and large lorries coming into Warners. It was a lovely surprise. After several weeks of being exposed we now had our privacy back!

When I pressed the door combination lock to go in, I found our first piece of mail lying on the mat. I was excited until I read who it was from! It was from the bungalow's old energy company wanting £10 for our final meter reading as we had now moved over to British Gas. It was a little disappointing, but at least we knew that mail was now getting through. Hopefully, next time it would be something exciting for us! Our friends prayed for us just before they left and went back to Peterborough.

That same day, I sent out some more letters to businesses and organisations locally asking them for their help and support with our project. We have to keep pressing on in faith.

On the last Wednesday of the year, Norman and I went down to the Centre to do further renovation work. Norman filled in a large hole in the fire room and I emulsioned the walls for the fourth time. The white wasn't covering the fire damage very well. Norman then went around the edges for me to finish it off. It was all coming along slowly and would look great when it was completed.

On the first Sunday of 2010, Mick at Warners texted me to say that a window had been broken at the front of our bungalow and there was an abandoned car parked in our driveway. Of course, Norman and I went straight round to have a look. Two windows were smashed, and sure enough there was a silver Astra in our driveway. We went straight into our tunnel area (the bit in between the two bungalows where we stored items such as the boards which were on all the windows etc) to get one of the boards to put it back on the window. We had a look inside the bungalow before we left, just to make sure there was nothing stolen or broken. Thankfully there wasn't. We just had some more glass to clean up! Afterwards, we went back home to inform the police. I gave them all the information I could and left it to them to do the rest.

One of the items of post on the mat was a great encouragement to me. It was from a small local business. I had written to Fitzgerald's Beds in Bourne asking if they could help us with some mattresses and single beds. His letter said that he would be willing to help us in any way he could and wanted to have a chat with me about this. It was such encouraging news, especially coming after the break-in.

On the first Wednesday of the new year, Amanda and I went to visit The Haven in Lincoln. It was similar to The Well Head Centre. We thought it might help us to see how others make it work. It was a place to which people with mental health problems were referred in the Lincoln area. Norman was planning on coming with us but he was ill so couldn't make it. Alison had also planned on coming but two of her children were taken ill and were very poorly, so there was just the two of us. Some snow had fallen the night before and I heard that Lincoln had about four inches so we were unsure as to go or not. So, we phoned the Haven, and also called our daughter to ask what the conditions were like. We decided we would make the trip. We were so glad we did as we had a wonderful time. The roads were fine too. We were given loads of good advice regarding things that we needed to do before we opened The Well Head Centre. One of the things they told us was that we needed to train the volunteers. This was something I hadn't even considered!

When we got back to Bourne I popped in to the Centre to measure the hallway in The Healing Rooms end, as a kind gentleman from church who owned a carpet business wanted to replace the carpet for us. Whilst I was there, I noticed all the left-over fencing and equipment had been removed from around the bungalow, so it looked much better for when people arrived for the official opening of The Healing Rooms.

Thursday 7 January was the official opening day. The weather was freezing, icy cold, with flurries of snow all day. People had been told not to go out unless it was really necessary. We had a brave team turn up that evening, giving us the perfect number ... seven! It was great. No-one came in for prayer so we prayed for one of our team. It was a good time to do this as we would have less time once we got busy. We had individual electric heaters in all the rooms. We were cosy and warm!

We presented all of the team members with their official Healing Rooms badges, so we looked the part! We had a great time of worship and praise. We took communion together and then prophesied Isaiah 61 over each other, 'The Spirit of the Lord is upon me.' We packed up and went home at 9.15pm. We look forward to all that God has got planned for The Healing Rooms, Bourne and beyond. God has made all this possible and we give Him all the praise and Glory.

Not another bill!

'I think you'd better see this,' I said handing Norman the bill from British Gas.

'£700! They've got to be kidding!'

The saga of the bills started on 8th January with British Gas and Total Gas & Power both claiming the same meter reading. It was quite ironic really as we hadn't actually had any gas, heating or hot water since we took over the bungalow! On 12 January I received a final demand for payment from Total Gas & Power. They said if I didn't pay, they would disconnect the supply and send me a bill for doing it despite the fact that they were supposed to have disconnected us on 8 December 2009!

On 19th January I opened the electricity bill for £700 mentioned above. I immediately phoned British Gas to see what was going on and afterwards phoned Mick at Warners to ask him if he could let me know the meter reading for his last bill. It seemed we had got some of his bill added to ours!

On Friday 29 January we received a water bill from Anglian Water for £482 for just four months. This seemed a bit extortionate as we had not been in the bungalow much, so I made some enquiries.

To add to the collection I received an electricity bill from EoN on 2nd February for £280 – a final demand for payment within five days or the debt collectors would be mobilised to come and get the money. Norman had a long conversation with them and they said they would sort this out. Our Directors Meeting for The Well Head Centre that evening was very timely. We discussed some urgent issues, and bills were our main concern!

The Council Tax bill arrived on 25th February which hadn't been paid since last October. So I gave it straight to Norman when he came in from work!

The stress of the situation was starting to get to me and I would wake up in the middle of the night, the bills going around my head. One morning after a bad night's sleep Linda from church called as she sensed there was something wrong. She prayed for me over the phone and said she sensed I had allowed a spirit of fear to come on me. I believe she was right as I had just been reading from my daily devotional by Kenneth and Gloria Copeland that fear can come in various ways without us even realising it and when I put the phone down, I also read about fear in *Stepping Stones to Freedom*.

God is really on my case. I always say to God that I need Him to tell me three times and then I know and I get it! He has done that this morning.

It wasn't just fear though. I had allowed the enormity of it all to get to me. I knew I had to stop, wait on the Lord, and let Him lead and not take all the responsibility on myself. And I needed to delegate a few of the things that I was doing to someone else to lighten my load. This was confirmed when my friend Tricia phoned me and gave me some words of wisdom from Exodus chapter 18 verses 18 to 20:

'Listen now to my voice, I will give you counsel and God will be with you: Stand before God for the people, so that you may bring the difficulties to God. And you shall teach them the statutes and the laws, and show them the way in which they must walk and the work they must do.'

It spoke to me about delegation – when Moses got a little weary, his father-in-law came to his aid. On 2nd February, I put these words into action and asked Norman if he would go to the Centre to take a reading of the water meter and I went off for a bit of retail therapy! In the evening I read the following email:

'You are not responsible for the success or failure of The Well Head Centre. You are not an island but part of a community, one (equal) member of a team that I have drawn together to fulfil My plans and purposes. I love your enthusiasm but do not let it consume you to the detriment of all the other blessings that I continue to shower upon you. Enjoy them! You thoroughly deserve them.'

And later another from a good friend at church: 'I was thinking about you a few moments ago and God prompted me to say to you that the problems you have encountered will be washed away, my faithful servant. Rest in My arms and let my peace cleanse you from the stresses that have been weighing you down. Psalm 18 is the Psalm that you should read also Psalm 46 is urged by God for you to read.'

That night I wrote in my journal:

> God is so good to me. He always sends someone along to encourage me when I am feeling down. I am reading loads of scriptures with promises in them. I need to just soak myself in the Word and trust Him.

The next day I wrote this:

> I slept until 7am this morning. How wonderful was that?! God is so good.

> I am still standing on God's promises. I read them every day to encourage me and to help me to trust Him completely with all that is going on in my life right now. It seems every book I pick up and every daily reading I read there is something which I need to take on board. God is definitely trying to tell me something. I need to continue trusting Him with all of my life and not try to work things out myself.

On 2nd March Alison and Niall (her husband) came round to help sort out three of the bills we had received. We had to decide what proportion should be paid by The Well Head Centre and what should be paid for by the Healing Rooms. We all agreed, and then wrote out the cheques ready to be posted. We were just waiting for EoN and Anglian Water to send us the amended bills and then we thought we would be back on track.

An envelope from EoN arrived on the doormat on 10th March – I was not looking forward to opening it. When I eventually did, to my surprise we had a bill with no amount to pay on it. ZERO payment. I was ecstatic. I waved it around thanking and praising God. We only had the enormous water bill to sort out after that, or so we thought.

On the 12th March we had another bill from British Gas for £427 for energy used from 10 February 2010–28 February 2010. I don't think so!

On 25th March I sent an email to British Gas stating that as they had not replied to my email on 13th March they left me with no choice. I would be stopping all direct debits and would contact Watchdog and the ombudsman to help us sort this mess out. I had a phone call at 4.30pm from one of the managers at British Gas. He was very apologetic. He told me he had done everything I had asked for in my email. I told him that I did not want any more estimated bills – I would send them the readings each month. As a gesture of goodwill he said he would credit our account with £50!!

On 30th March I received a British Gas bill based on our reading and it was much better than the other bills – only £103. Praise God.

On 17th April a letter arrived from Anglian Water. Neither of us could understand what it was saying as they had got all the dates muddled up. Two days later we received two more bills from them, over £500 each! Norman gave them a ring. After a long conversation the good news was that we would receive a revised bill later that week for £17!! So again, God is so good. After three months we had finally got all the bills sorted out.

The bills weren't our only headache at the time. We had no heating or hot water which, apart from anything else, made it difficult for the materials used for decorating, carpeting etc. to dry out. On 19th January three heating engineers spent most of the day trying to sort out the radiators but without success. Three days later the heating engineer put a new part in the boiler so we hoped we could at least get some hot water. Warners said they would sort out the radiators one by one over the following week. They would need to take the fronts off each one and spray the trip-switch with WD-40 to loosen them up.

On 6th February when we opened the gas meter room there was water coming out of the pipes in there. One of Warners engineers had a look and said it needed a new part so in the meantime he turned the water off and we couldn't use the toilet.

On 9th February two of Warners staff made a further attempt at fixing the heating. They took all twenty-three radiators off but still they hadn't cracked it! A week later there was no heating on in the bungalow at all and it was freezing. I phoned Mark and Mick at Warners but got no reply so I then texted them both. Mark gave me a call at about 4pm and said he would get Jim to go round and have a look and see what he could do. When we arrived at 6pm I think they had only been there for half an hour as it was still really cold. The temperature outside was zero degrees.

The heating continued to be intermittent and the pilot light kept going out on the boiler. In May a plumber came to look at the boiler room and the radiators to see if he could sort out the problem. He said he would give us a quote to fix the zone valve to stop the water going all around the other three bungalows before it gets to ours! Warners said they would pay to have the radiators fixed if the quote was good. (More on this in the next chapter.)

In the meantime we had quite a lot of things we needed to change or implement in The Well Head Centre but I believed with God's provision we would do it. One of our first priorities was to get all the broken windows at the front of the bungalow repaired as soon as possible and to put some signs up so that people would think the building was occupied. This might help to deter vandals, the fire officers advised. In February Norman put up two sets of Venetian blinds at the front windows and Gerald and Peter replaced the three broken window panes. Gerald also put up some hanging baskets to make it look more homely and lived in from the outside.

In April we had a further visit from the Fire Officer. 'If you want to keep two of the six bedrooms you'll need to move this set of double doors six feet along the corridor,' he said. 'Fire safety rules, I'm afraid.' This seemed to be yet another setback, but God was ready to intervene. Later that day a gentleman called Peter had just been in the Healing

Rooms for ministry and he wanted to come and have a look around the bungalow to see what we were doing. I told him about needing to move the doors and he said 'That's easy!'

'Is it?' I said.

'Yes. I'm a master carpenter; I can do that easily. It wouldn't take me long.'

I also told him that we needed a door putting in the wall so that we could get into our new shower room and he agreed to do that too. When I went to get the wood for him from our friend who has a wood yard, he gave it to us FREE OF CHARGE. God is so good.

Lots of other people offered their help too. In January Gerald wallpapered one of the walls in the fire room using a black embossed wallpaper to cover the horrible mess on the wall where the fire had been and a load of grease and Mick fitted a new carpet in there.

A friend at KingsGate Community Church who owns a carpet shop in Peterborough offered to have a fitter come and carpet the corridor in the Healing Rooms. It wasn't an easy job as the old carpet was stuck to the floor. When he eventually got it all up, the glue for the new carpet wasn't setting as the bungalow was so cold. But he went ahead and did it anyway and it looked great! Keith from church assembled a brand-new six-foot desk he donated to us for the entrance to the Healing Rooms. When he'd finished it looked like a proper reception area – really professional. Some weeks later we added some finishing touches. We hung all the Directors' and Associate Directors' certificates on the wall and a gorgeous picture of a bridge where two different waters meet. It is a fitting depiction of our two charities (The Healing Rooms and The Well Head Centre) blending.

With so many jobs to complete, we decided to have a decorating week in March. Gerald, Amanda and Natalie came to help on the first day. Our first task was to try to get the brown, sticky mastic off the new panes of glass. We tried petrol, Windowlene and plastic scrapers but it was slow work. Then Gerald had a brainwave. 'We need a Stanley knife. Shame I didn't bring one.'

'You didn't but Norman did!' I said brandishing one from his toolbox.

Five windows and one door later we were ready for lunch. We tucked in to soup and bread rolls, cheese and coleslaw sandwiches and grapes, biscuits and chocolate Brazil nuts.

After that we moved more furniture into one bedroom ready for decorating, cleaned out the large chest freezer and painted two radiators and skirting boards in one of the rooms. On Monday six people came to help decorate. As we started to transform those bedrooms, I believed it was in preparation for God to transform lives:

Some of the rooms will just need a lick of paint and some of the holes filling in and then they will be ready. Some will need to be totally gutted, stripped back to the bare walls. I believe God is saying this is like the transformation that will happen in those who will be staying here. Some will be relatively easy to help to get back on track but others will need extra love, care and compassion to rebuild their broken lives.

I believe also that God has spoken two promises over The Well Head Centre today and I claim them both: Isaiah 60 verse 21 'They shall inherit the land forever' and Isaiah 61 verse 7 'Therefore in the land they shall possess double.'

The following day we had ten helpers in the day and three more in the evening. Praise God. The horrible dirty pink walls of the long corridor were now clean and bright thanks to Pete Kelly who had tirelessly been decorating every week.

On Wednesday Sarah from church came down to help with the painting and ironing. We managed to get one more curtain up in the lounge. Alison's daughter Catherine also popped by to mark out some things in the quad area.

Also that week Mark (our electrician) sorted out the wall lights in our lounge and the electrics in the office. On Saturday his wife Gill joined him and helped me sort out some curtains in the store room. She ended up taking a pair of green curtains home with her to shorten and wash for me so we could use them in the twin room.

I did a lot of (white) gloss painting – radiators and bedrooms and undercoated all the paintwork in one of the bedrooms where previously it had been blue!

More valuable help arrived on Friday 26th March from my hygienist friend, Gill. We met at 10.30am and started sorting out the storeroom, a job I had put off doing. There were bags and boxes of all kinds of stuff that many kind people had given to us when they heard about our project. We sorted out towels, curtains, duvets, pillows, lamps and wallpaper that we wanted to keep. We then had four bags left over ready to go to the Salvation Army Charity shop along with a three-piece suite. I couldn't have done this job on my own and felt so blessed to have such good friends. God is so good.

One day in mid-April I was feeling a little despondent as not much was going on at The Well Head Centre. No new volunteers. No money coming in for the bathroom and en suite. So I asked the Lord to bring me some encouragement. About half an hour later I received a text from my electrician friend Mark. He had been collecting a few things for me – a shower screen and tray, some paint, curtain poles and other stuff and wanted to drop them off.

* * *

On 17 May our carpet fitter laid some new bedroom carpet and some hard-wearing carpet to go by the front door as well as a spare piece of brown carpet in the office. We now had three lots of new carpet in the bungalow, all free of charge, and it was beginning to smell so much sweeter!

That evening I met the builder and plumber who were coming to give us a quote for the bathroom, shower room and two en suites. On their way out, the plumber saw the mess the laundry room was in and said he would sort it out for us. I asked him to do it on a separate quote but he said he would do it for nothing. Bless God. He has all this in hand. I don't need to worry or be anxious.

We experienced many other gifts in kind that Spring including the Salvation Army Officer and his wife offering to buy a brand-new tumble dryer for the Centre, a lady from Lincolnshire CVS being willing to train our volunteers for FREE and a lady who, after receiving prayer ministry asked us if we needed any turf for the garden. Of course, we said yes to all these offers. Alison's daughter Catherine was particularly chuffed about the turf as a couple of weeks earlier she had mentioned that the grass was not very good in the quad area. She had agreed to work on our garden as part of her project at school.

That year we had been hearing a lot about God's grace, His unmerited favour. I wanted to position myself to receive His grace. On 14th February Norman and I went to the Wyevale Garden Centre in Crowland for lunch. The queue was long and slow but we both kept saying 'grace and more grace' to each other as we waited to get our lunch. When we finally got to the counter to choose what we wanted, the beef had all gone but they were just bringing out a large joint of gammon. It looked wonderful, so we both decided we would have that instead. Just at that point the manager came up behind us and said 'You can let this last couple have their meal free today as we have worked non-stop since 12.15pm.' It was now about 2.20pm. We just looked at each other and smiled and then turned to the manager and said 'Well thank you so much and be blessed.' Later that day our son Glyn phoned and asked if we had had our dessert yet as Katherine (our daughter in law) had made a lemon meringue pie. We said 'No' but I told him about our free lunch and he said 'Well now you can have a free dessert!' So all the family came round and we shared dessert together. What an amazing day. God is so good. It is wonderful to live and walk in His grace. I want to stay there forever. Bless God.

Another thing I had been learning about was sowing and reaping. I had been reading *A Daily Guide to Miracles* by Oral Roberts. He talks about sowing a seed for your miracle – financial, physical, material, spiritual or whatever. We must give God something to work with. So on 20th March we planted a seed and put some money into The Well Head Centre bank account to receive our financial miracle. The following Wednesday we received a cheque for £1000. I wrote in my journal:

> God is so good. Norman and I sowed a financial seed into The Well Head Centre last Friday and we have received £1250 in donations this week. Talk about sowing and reaping. This is more than a tenfold or

twelvefold return! Our God is so faithful to His Word. I feel like I want to sow even more now! I feel we are on our way. He is Jehovah Jireh. He will provide. Nothing is too difficult for Him. He is our Amazing God.

Following on from this, a few weeks later Amanda phoned me with an encouraging scripture:

'But by an equality, that now at this time your abundance may supply their lack, that their abundance may supply your lack – that there may be equality' (2 Corinthians 8:14).

Thank you Lord! We have a God of abundance. There is no lack in Him. I believe that when we have an abundance of stuff we don't need, we can pass it on to others in their lack. Like the three-piece suite and other things out of our storeroom that we don't need.

As well as financial blessing, God was bringing the right people along to volunteer at the Centre. Sarah, a friend who helped on the decorating week was one of those people. She told me her heart just lately had been for the broken and hurting and she was asking the Lord to reveal to her how she could reach out to them. She had been having dreams and visions of a large house in the country where people would come and stay for a while, like a retreat, then go back home – exactly what we will be doing at The Well Head Centre. We had a great time sharing our dreams and visions – and a few tears – together. When two people connect with the same heart to see God's purposes being done, it really humbles you and joins you together in Him.

Early in the year I contacted The Len Pick Trust, an organisation that helps local charities and organisations with funding. They arranged to meet us at the centre on Friday 19 March. After we had showed them around they explained that they would need certain things to be in place before they would consider supporting us financially. The key one was whether we were going to ask the GPs in town to refer guests to us. They also wanted to know what donations we had received and about training our volunteers. Following on from their meeting to discuss our grant application we received a letter from them to say they didn't feel they could help us at this time. They wanted us to jump through a lot more hoops for them to be satisfied that we fitted their criteria. I was disappointed but wrote in my journal:

God will provide. I know He will. We keep praying and keep believing that He will provide the provision for the vision.

In April we went to a Funding Fair in Grantham and met Tamsin and Mary from the County Council who wanted to help us if they could. In May, Mary came to see us to discuss funding. She was brilliant and knew exactly the right people and places we needed to get in touch with. We decided to go for a grant of £500 for printing costs and one for £2,000 for the bathroom and shower room. Mary would also look into 'Awards for All' to see if we qualified for £10,000.

We also began the process of contacting those who might be able to refer people to us. I posted two letters to the GP practices in Bourne and we met up with Annie, a district nurse in West Deeping to see if she could go to the GPs on our behalf and talk to them about The Well Head Centre. She was excited about what we were planning to do and helped us to restructure our Referral Criteria. Nevertheless, I felt a little overawed about going to speak to the doctors in town. It seemed too big for me to achieve. I thought of how Moses must have felt when God told him to speak to the Israelites in Egypt. He said, 'Who am I?' I felt just like that. The doctors would want to know who I am and I needed to know how to answer that question.

Soon after having these thoughts I picked up *A Daily Guide to Miracles* and read the next chapter. Well, I laughed and cried at the same time. Everything I had prayed was in this one chapter. This is what I wrote in my journal:

God's timing is always perfect. Moses was saying that he stuttered and that he wasn't the right person to be doing this. This is exactly what I had been telling God a few minutes earlier. He showed Moses a miracle with the staff he had in his hand. It turned into a snake. Well I need something new to convince me that I am the right person to do all that needs to be done. The final sentence of this chapter reads 'God is alive, and continually active in my life.' I really need to take hold of that and do what God has called me to do. I believe I have to be upfront and let them know that this is God's idea and He is in charge. I do not go in my own strength. He will be with me. I believe he will go before me and prepare the way for me and they will listen, hear and will want to support this project. Praise God.

I was further encouraged when I spoke to a GP from church. He gave me some valuable information about GPs which I wrote down. The following Wednesday I had an excuse to see my doctor as I had sore ankles. While there I told her about the Centre and she was very interested. She said she would pass my letter on to the Practice Manager and she would also bring it up at their next meeting. I was relieved to have had such a positive response!

* * *

Our prayer team were a vital support throughout the project. At the beginning of March I sent out the new prayer pointers along with a letter entitled 'Sow an Acorn'. We were asking all those on our Prayer Support Team to consider giving £10 a month to help finance The Well Head Centre. At the end of the month I was a little disappointed with the response. No one had taken us up on this request for finances. However, it wasn't long before two people and then a couple said they would like to sow an acorn. I believed this would be the start of the financial flow into this project.

God encouraged me countless times that year through Scripture, words and prayers. On Tuesday 23 March I wrote in my journal:

I believe the Lord gave me Deuteronomy 28:7-12 today as confirmation for all we are doing in The Well Head Centre. We will possess the land.

'The LORD your God will bless you in the land He is giving you ... The LORD will grant you abundant prosperity – in the fruit of your womb, the young of your livestock and the crops of your ground – in the land he swore to your forefathers to give you. The LORD will open the heavens, the storehouse of His bounty, to send rain on your land in season and to bless the work of your hands.'

At this moment in time, we have only been promised the bungalow until September 2013 but I believe God is preparing the way for us to have it permanently. When agencies and organisations come to have a look around, they get a bit cautious about giving us financial help, as we may not be here in four years' time. We find it quite hard to get them to think the way we think! So I thank God for His confirmation to me this morning from His Word.

On Tuesday 6 April I wrote:

In the Healing Rooms we are receiving more and more testimonies via our website and prayer requests from all over the world, it is so amazing. We are also sending 'Prayer Cloths' all over the world too. People are getting healed, praise God.

I read 1 Chronicles 28:20-21 today. It really is a wonderful scripture and I have taken hold of its promises for The Well Head Centre.

'And David said to his son Solomon, be strong and of good courage, and do it; do not fear or be dismayed for the LORD God, my God, will be with you. He will not leave you nor forsake you, until you have finished all the work for the service of the house of

the LORD. Here are the divisions of the priests and the Levites for all the service of the house of God; and every willing craftsman will be with you for all manner of workmanship, for every kind of service, also the leaders and all the people will be completely at your command.'

Sunday 25 April was a particularly significant day. As I was having my quiet time with the Lord I asked Him for a scripture. I opened my Bible to Isaiah 60. This is an amazing passage. Verse 1 says:

'Arise, shine for your light has come! And the glory of the LORD is risen upon you. For behold, the darkness shall cover the earth, and deep darkness the people. But the LORD will arise over you, and His glory will be seen upon you.'

When church had finished, we went to lunch in Crowland with a couple of friends. On the way there I just started shouting and praising God saying 'Thank you Lord for the local funding body refusing to help us financially – I feel free. I don't feel restricted anymore. My feet are not shackled anymore. Freedom, freedom, freedom! We don't need to solely concentrate on the Bourne area. We can go further afield, praise God. Thank you Lord that I have liberty and freedom.' I was so excited. I think Norman was taken aback for a while with my outburst! But it had to come out!

While we were having lunch our friends said they knew two Christian doctors where they lived and would get in touch with them and pass their names on to us. I felt we were back on track. The floodgates would open up and we would see the glory of the Lord in this place.

When I finally decided to go to bed, I went into the bathroom and noticed something glistening all over one wall. I had to take a closer look and I ran my hand all over the wall to see what it was. I got it on my hands and I kept going over it and it just kept coming back more and more. I believe it was gold dust. I hadn't actually seen gold dust before but I was sure that this was it. I shouted to Norman upstairs to see what he thought it could be. He first said he thought it could be the glitter off my hairspray but I hadn't used it for three weeks. I believe it was yet another sign to me from the Lord.

It was still there the next morning. When I told Hazel and Malcolm (great friends of ours) about the two rejected grant applications and the gold dust Hazel said it was in the bathroom because this was where we needed the finances – money to convert the bathroom, shower room and two en suites in the Centre. I hadn't thought of that but I believe she was right. This was a sign from God letting us know that the money would be on its way. Praise God for His provision.

Wednesday 28 April: There is still gold dust in the bathroom!

On Saturday 1 May I read in my daily reading book 'Delay is not denial'. I really needed to hear that. It went on to explain why it seems God delays answering our prayers but that his timing is always perfect.

Exciting family matters that year included Hazel and Matt announcing Hazel being pregnant with her third child and Norman's retirement. Norman had been considering retirement for a couple of years then on Thursday 11 February he told me that he sensed God had released him from full-time employment and it was finally time to retire. I was so pleased to hear this news. He had been at South Holland District Council for twenty-eight years. But now he would have the opportunity to do other things and to serve God in new ways.

His last day in the office was 13 April and the following afternoon we went over to our daughter and son-in-laws for a family gathering, a 'Retirement Tea' followed by a sleepover. A couple of days later we went on the local bus to Peterborough (about one hour away) to book our holiday to America.

Several difficult things happened to our family in May that reminded us of our need to cover everything in prayer. In May Hazel's husband Matt was physically attacked by one of the patients on the mental health ward he works on. He received a bump to the head and had been punched, battered and bruised before other members of staff came to help him. The previous week another patient had bitten his shoulder and he had to have a tetanus injection as it was a messy bite. Also, their five-year-old son Zach was at his swimming lesson but the water was too cold for him (the boiler had broken) and he started to go blue and lifeless in the water. Thankfully, the teacher dragged him out of the pool and she and Hazel managed to revive him.

We all believe that this is an attack from the enemy because of what we are about to embark on at The Well Head Centre, mental health issues included. We are now praying for total protection for our families 24/7. We are all on a learning curve as we go deeper into God's plans and purposes.

At the end of May we went to the Healing Rooms Conference in Halifax. While we were there a lady had a picture of a well head out at sea (like an oil rig) and the top had been capped, but now the cap had been taken off and everything was gushing out of the top of it! The lady said it was water gushing out, but Amanda said it was oil and it was burning very brightly. Then Mary said it was gold. We were so excited about this word and we took it for us at The Well Head Centre. Praise God for another confirmation.

* * *

One of the highlights of 2010 was our holiday in June in Yosemite National Park in California. We saw some amazing sights. The scenery was truly breath taking and the mountains were incredible. Everything was so BIG: the mountains, the trees, the waterfalls – my neck ached because everything was so high! I reflected on this a few months later after reading this question from *Streams in the Desert*: 'Are you willing to sacrifice to reach the glorious mountain peaks of God's purpose for you?'

If I am to reach those glorious mountain peaks of God's purposes for me, it is not going to be an easy path but I know it is going to be worth it. My life is in His hands. If The Well Head Centre is successful, then God gets the glory. If it fails, then it is still God's. It is not about me; it's all about Him. I am learning to trust Him so much more by going through this. I realise how good He is to me.

Birth pangs

I feel like Moses when he found himself on the edge of the Red Sea with nowhere else to go! We have now got to a stage where there is nothing moving. We have no GPs willing to refer people to us. We have no builders' quotes that we can realistically submit. We have no finances to pay the cost of the jobs which are needed to be done. We are now at a standstill waiting on God to tell us what to do next.

I wrote these words in my journal in July after receiving two bombshells: a letter from the GPs here in Bourne saying that they were unable to refer people to us as we were not registered with the NHS and a quote from a builder to complete the bathroom, shower room plus two en suites for £12,000. We really needed a miracle to get this project up and running now.

Following on from this several encouraging things happened. I received an email from a lady called Jeni who we met in America at Bethel Church.

Hi Janice

Praying for you and your family an increase in favour for all that you need, for strength and protection, boldness and courage, complete trust in Him!...When I prayed for you a few weeks ago I had a picture of you walking on very hot sand which meant you had to walk quickly. It was fine and soon your feet got used to it but I almost felt the Lord doesn't want you comfortable(!) He is always after the expansion of His Kingdom and so The Well Head is a start but it's just the start! I know you know that but felt I should let you know about the comfortable bit!! Also I saw a brain with all the nerve endings sparking, some connecting and some not. Felt again and probably quite obvious, some connections may look right but they won't quite fit, so am praying that you will have eyes to see those God connections and not waste time on other ones! Loved meeting you in California . . . . Had such a great time. Loads of love, Jeni x

That evening at the Trustees meeting we signed the Constitution we had recently drawn up which meant we could proceed with the funding applications. Then Alison had an inspired thought – perhaps pastors of churches could refer people to us. This seemed to just click in my spirit. Health professionals seemed a bit cautious about referring people to us, (understandably) so this might be a better idea to pursue and pray about.

I also read the following from *Streams in the Desert*. It was entitled 'Be Men of Courage, Be Strong'.

'Never pray for an easier life – pray to be a stronger person! Never pray for tasks equal to your power – pray for power equal to your tasks! Then doing your work will be no miracle – you will be the miracle!

We must remember that Christ will not lead us to greatness through an easy or self-indulgent life. An easy life does not lift us up but only takes us down. Heaven is always above us and we must continually be looking toward it. Some people always avoid things that are costly or things that require self-denial, self-restraint and self-sacrifice, yet it is hard work, and difficulties that ultimately lead us to greatness. For greatness is not found by walking the moss-covered path laid out for us through the meadow. It is found by being sent to carve out our own path with our own hands'[1]

---

1 . Taken from *Streams in the Desert* by LB Cowman and Copyright © 1997 by LB Cowman. Used by permission of HarperCollins Christian Publishing. www.harpercollinschristian.com

The image of Moses standing at the Red Sea stayed with me. I wanted to go to the seaside, stand at the water's edge, look out over the expanse of sea, and wait on the Lord for direction. Amanda was keen to do this too so she, Norman and I went to Holkham Beach (in Norfolk) on 7th August. As we were walking towards the beach it started spitting with rain and lots of people started to leave. We were not deterred. Norman opened up his folding chair and sat himself down. Amanda stripped off her outer clothing and went straight into the sea for a swim. I rolled up my shorts, took my shoes and socks off and gently stepped in to the cool but strangely clear water. I noticed calmness where I was standing, but on both sides of me there were rolling waves. Then I looked up and saw a bit of blue sky above us and eventually the sun came out. When Amanda came back from her swim, she noticed the calmness of the sea where we were standing and the window of heaven open above us too. We believed God was saying we didn't need to worry about a thing. We were in calm waters. The window of heaven is God's favour and protection over us. We are His. He will never leave us or forsake us and He has everything under His control.

Meanwhile, the practical tasks continued. The 17th August was a particularly productive day. Peter, the qualified carpenter I mentioned in the last chapter moved the set of double doors eight feet up the corridor to include two of the bedrooms, in case of fire. When Norman and I popped in on our way to the Healing Rooms in the evening, to our amazement, they looked beautiful. You wouldn't have known that they weren't there before!

Peter Hubbard screwed The Well Head Centre and Healing Rooms signs to the outside wall at the front and back of the bungalow, Peter K emulsioned the kitchen ceiling and Norman undercoated the front door. Margaret, Natalie and I picked apples and plums off the fruit trees. There was an abundance of fruit; it was glorious and seemed to be prophetic for the fruitfulness of Healing Rooms and The Well Head Centre.

I do feel at this time we are about to birth something. We have been preparing the bungalow since January of this year. It is now August. I believe we need to make one final push in the next few weeks to birth this project.

* * *

I realised just recently that we have three Peters helping us in The Well Head Centre. Peter H, Peter K and Peter D. The name Peter in the Bible means 'the rock'. I always ask God to show me three times if He wants me to get something, then I get it! So I believe the three Peters are helping us to build firm foundations for The Well Head Centre and the Healing Rooms. 'Unless the LORD builds the house, they labour in vain, those who build it' (Psalm 127:1). The Well Head Centre and the Healing Rooms are built on the rock. We have a firm foundation. Praise God.

At the end of August, we decided to embark on a forty-day prayer and fast from 1 September to 10 October alongside our church. We needed to seek God on some specific areas in The Well Head Centre and encouraged all those on our Prayer Support Team to partner with us to see mighty breakthroughs here in Bourne.

We also met up with Mary (the lady from the County Council who we had connected with at the Grantham Funding Fair) and Ruth. Mary helped us put the finishing touches to two grant applications. One for £500 for printing and stationery costs and one for £2,000 for the bathroom and shower room costs (we decided not to pursue the two ensuites). Ruth was helping us with our policies for The Centre. How we needed this kind of help. I was disappointed when I received a letter a month later to say we had been declined any funding for stationery costs.

However, we were encouraged in other ways. From July to November, we held training events for all our volunteers on Listening Skills, First Aid, Health and Safety and Food Hygiene, plus Fire Risk booked in for the following January. Most of the volunteers also completed their CRB checks. We were all pleasantly surprised by how much we enjoyed the courses and had a good laugh at some of the horrendous stories related to food hygiene!

We felt particularly blessed at the First Aid course as the LIVES Doctor who came was a Christian and said he would be interested in referring guests to us. He also gave Norman the name and address of a Mental Health Chaplain in Sleaford, said he would do some follow-up training free of charge and would send us some extra bits to put in our First Aid box.

By the end of the year, we had twenty-four volunteers, enthusiastic and committed to the project and ready to go.

Others started to offer their services for when The Wellhead Centre would be finally up and running. Andrea who does my nails volunteered to come and do some beauty therapy treatment on our guests – nails, back massage, eyebrows, facial etc. And Louise, my massage therapist said that she would like to come and do massages once a month for our guests free of charge (FOC)! Wow! I was shocked and surprised. God was really moving fast and he knew what we needed! Amanda had got chatting to a pianist called Graham Tickle who regularly plays for the afternoon tea at the George Hotel, in Stamford. She was there with her mother-in-law who has dementia and finds the music soothing. He was very interested in The Well Head Centre so she asked him if he would be willing to come and play for our guests some time. He said he would love to come and would bring his own keyboard.

Interestingly this happened on the final day of our forty-day prayer and fast. I wrote in my journal:

God is setting up a programme for all our guests. I believe we shall see many breakthroughs from today. Things that were hard will now be easy. Ways that were blocked will now be opened in front of us. Financial breakthrough will come. Even more favour will flow. There will be an open heaven now and the blessings will flow. The anointing will flow. My hand aches now with writing all this down but it is all so exciting. To top it all at the end of the day, I stood in my bathroom at home and saw gold dust on the walls again. God is so faithful. He is truly amazing. What would I ever do without Him?

In early September we went to a Christian camping event in Lincoln called Grapevine. I bought a book there by Rachel Hickson called *Eat the Word – Speak the Word*. The cover alone is amazing – a large spoon with syrup pouring down from it! Rachel was at the event so I asked her if she wouldn't mind signing the book for me. She said she would be delighted. Not only did she sign it, she put a word in it for me too:

'You carry grace and compassion for many, so let your heart of service flow, but be ready to speak the word of freedom and wisdom. You are made to carry freedom.'

WOW! I was amazed and thrilled. She also said to me, 'I see you carrying a flag and waving it around, and whilst you are waving it, you are cutting people free and releasing them into their freedom.'

Well, that was amazing too, as I had recently picked up our new banner made from beautiful purple, blue and pink iridescent material and had waved it around in the Healing Rooms. It wasn't like me to do that sort of thing, but I had really felt the urge to do it.

On the last day of the event, we were asked if we wanted to go forward for prayer and a fresh anointing and to be used more by God. Norman and I went out to the front. After we had received prayer and were turning around to go back to our seats, a lady (who I vaguely knew from KingsGate Church) came up to me and said, 'What's this about a bathroom?' I told her the story so far and that we needed £2,000 to fit out a bathroom and shower room. She said, 'Well I sense God has asked me to give you £2,000. There may be more, if not in money, but in time. We want to help you.' Well, I was flabbergasted! I hugged her and cried. If ever we needed confirmation that God would supply all that we needed for this project, this was it. A few days later I was very excited to receive the cheque from her.

We came back to reality with a bit of a bang – our computer crashed, BIG time. We had been infected with twelve viruses and it took us, and our son Glyn, nearly a week to sort it out. Glyn said we needed to invest in a new computer as this one was too slow!

* * *

One major piece of work that had not yet been tackled at the bungalow was the laundry room, particularly the removal of a large, smelly sluice. On Tuesday 7 September Peter H brought his friend Bob who is an electrician and plumber to help sort this out. But when they tried removing the sluice, loads of water came gushing out! Peter came to fetch me out of Healing Rooms worship to ask me where the stopcock was. First, we turned off the water meter tap in the street. That didn't work. Then we turned off the tap in the meter room in the garden. That didn't work either. A guy from Warners came to the rescue and took Peter and Bob into the loft space in the boiler room to show them where the taps were. They turned the taps off but still had to drain off all the water in the system – for all four bungalows as they are all connected! It took absolutely ages. When it finally stopped, they removed the sluice and discovered that none of the connections to the pipes worked properly so Peter had to buy about ten replacements. They worked very hard and did a great job. Thankfully when we turned the water back on to make sure it was safe, there were no leaks!

* * *

We were in Sheddy's Fish and Chip Restaurant in Spalding enjoying the most scrumptious fish, chips and mushy peas ever when I noticed a man at the table opposite me who was all alone. He seemed to be wiping tears away from his face. I thought 'Oh no, not another one.' I continued to watch him trying to wipe away the tears without anyone noticing. Then I told Norman and he turned around to have a look at him. He was now crying uncontrollably with his face bent down into his hands. I was really upset. I wasn't sure if I should go over to investigate or not but I didn't get the go-ahead from Norman so once we'd finished our food we left. I felt awful all the way home because I had done nothing. I repented and asked God to forgive me if I had missed His promptings. When I got home, I prayed for the man. I don't know if I had done the right thing but I do know God was showing me a hurting world and that we couldn't just walk away. I wanted another chance. I have to give away all that God has deposited in me.

On Tuesday 21 September in my prayer time before Healing Rooms I waited to hear what God wanted to impart to me. I did not want to move until He blessed me! I then thanked Him that I had received what I had asked for and went off to the Healing Rooms. During worship I seemed to be getting hotter and hotter and more and more vocal! We were praying for people to be set free from bondages and that chains would be broken off them. I really felt that some of the team needed this. I went around every person breaking off chains and bondages and setting them all free in the name of Jesus. I just had to do it. I had no choice. Then the teams got ready for ministry and intercession and I put myself on reception. While I was waiting for the people to go in and out of the ministry rooms, I read Jeremiah 33:3: 'Call to Me, and I will answer you and show you great and mighty things which you do not know.'

The Kingdom Dynamics in my Bible related to this said:

'God promised Jeremiah that if he would call to Him, not only would He answer him but He would reveal to him great and mighty things that could not otherwise be known. The word "mighty" is better rendered "isolated" or "inaccessible." The suggestion is that God would give Jeremiah "revelational insight", revealing things that otherwise would be inaccessible or isolated. Such revelational insight always has been essential for a clear understanding of victorious spiritual warfare. One cannot pray effectively without insight into how to pray, as well as into what things God truly longs for us to seek after in prayer.'

In my prayer time I had said that I didn't want to pray 'off-pat' prayers anymore but specific, strategic, personal prayers for everyone. I believe God showed me in His word that He had imparted 'revelational insight' to me.

At the end of September as I was walking down the high street, I noticed some wicker chairs in the window of the Salvation Army Charity Shop. I had been asking God for six chairs, one for each of the bedrooms. These were quite ornate with an interesting pattern on them and I thought they would look good in our bedrooms – and there were six of them. I tried one out and it was really comfortable. I then told the assistant who I was and why I needed them. She went to phone the Salvation Army Officer and when she came back, she said I could have all of them free of charge! Funnily enough I had spoken to someone from the Salvation Army the night before and I had told him that I was looking for six wicker chairs. Well, as I was coming out of the shop, I met him and he said, 'Have you seen the wicker chairs in the window?' I said, 'Yes, I have just got them!' God was really on my case!

* * *

At church on Sunday 3 October a lady prayed for me and had a picture. She saw a well (funnily enough!) with the head of it blocked up. Then she saw the lid come off and there were springs bubbling up and coming over the top with water flowing everywhere. Then she saw some gates open wide, and Jesus dancing and being so excited about all that was happening. She was laughing at Jesus being so happy. It was great. I was so encouraged. When she had finished, I reminded her that our project was called The Well Head Centre and she said that she had forgotten. How amazing! God is so good. She also said that Jesus was pleased with everything and my faithfulness in it. And not to worry about a thing; there will be an ease in it all. This also confirms what the people at Bethel Church, California prayed over me and Norman when we were there. I trust Him completely.

The same day Alison told me about a gentleman in her church who goes over to Latvia frequently to take supplies to the Blue Cross

Church there. In this church they look after homeless men who have been on drugs or alcohol or have just come out of prison. They accommodate around two hundred in their church at one time. At that moment they were trying to raise £2,100 to buy a new central heating boiler as theirs has broken down and could not be fixed. The temperature reaches below minus twenty-seven degrees at times and so they desperately needed a new boiler. 'Do you think it would make sense for us to sow a seed into this church to help them get their new boiler?' Alison asked. 'I just think we will then receive what we are believing God for – the heating, all the radiators working properly and the bathroom and shower room fully fitted out and usable.' Norman and I thought this was a brilliant idea so I emailed all the Trustees to see what they thought.

They all agreed so at the next Trustees meeting I wrote a cheque out for £500 and as soon as our meeting had finished Norman and I took it round to the guy from the Baptist church. I was so excited and expectant of what God was going to do. I stayed in the car as Norman went to the front door. He seemed to take ages. Eventually he came back – he still had the envelope with him! 'They had received all the money they needed and didn't need our contribution,' he said. I was a little upset and thought that we had got it all wrong. As Norman and I talked we both then believed that we hadn't got it wrong, we had got it right; we were just being obedient and we shall receive all that we need for our project too.

* * *

'I think I've come up with an affordable solution to the bathroom and shower room,' Mark informed me. 'If you can arrange a meeting with Phil and Peter, I'll explain it then.' It sounded promising so on 5th October we all met in the old bathroom to discuss how we could convert one large room into two smaller ones to accommodate a shower room too. We needed to erect a dividing wall and to put in a door on the wall along the corridor to allow people to get into the shower room. After a good discussion we all came to the same conclusion: it was achievable and affordable. Mark would price everything up and get back to me. A week later Mark had got hold of a basin and pedestal for the bathroom and had ordered all the other materials we needed. He told me he could start the work the week commencing 8 November and it would cost £2,000.

Satisfied with the solution to the bathroom, we continued to work on the other rooms. We put our first bed up in one of the bedrooms and added a bedside table and a lamp. It looked beautiful. The headboard and curtain rail are black wrought iron. The lampshades are cream and everything matches and goes well together.

One of our friends had got a bed he wanted to deliver to us and the friendly bed shop owner in Bourne said that he would be more than willing to supply two single beds and four mattresses free of charge!

I had been praying about what we should call each of the bedrooms at The Well Head Centre. Up to that point we had named them after the colour of the emulsion that we painted the walls with – Blue Room, Orange Room, White Room and Yellow Room. For the last couple of weeks, I had heard about, read about or actually seen a rainbow, so I believed God was confirming to me to keep the rooms named by the colours we had painted them. As people walk through the colours of the rainbow, it signifies God's promises to us forever.

On Thursday 21 October I wrote in my journal:

> Early this morning I asked God to bring me some encouragement today. I recalled when we were at Bethel Church, California last June, we were both told that when we got back home it was going to be easy! Well to be honest it has been quite difficult at times. So I was just reminding God about this. Things seem to take so long to come about and I can get a bit frustrated and start to question myself. Then I take it to God and get Him back on my case and I feel much better about things.

Not long after, Peter our friendly carpenter, let me know about hiring cutting equipment to make a doorway in the wall for the shower room and Phil the plumber said he would come to remove the radiator out of the bathroom. Bless God! He always hears my cries.

On 25th October I wrote in my journal:

> I am learning to trust God so much more as I am involved in this amazing project. I still don't quite know why God chose me to do this for Him. He reveals to me more and more that He has got everything under His control and I need not be anxious about anything. Many times I have prayed, spoken or just thought about something we need when someone comes along and asks if I need that very thing! For instance, last week I had been saying to the Lord that we will need some Bibles in every bedroom. I thought that I would get in touch with the Gideons but the next day Margaret came into The Healing Rooms with some (Gideon) Bibles. How amazing is that?

On another occasion we found a box of cream tiles in the storeroom with just the right number for Peter to finish tiling around the sink unit in the laundry room. Then there was Norman's brainwave about the locks on all the bedroom doors. 'Some doors like the laundry room, storeroom and kitchen/dining room don't need locks,' he said, so we moved those locks onto the bedroom doors. Plus, we have the two spare ones Peter found in the box in the shed.' We had saved ourselves about a thousand pounds. All we needed was a master key to get into all of them!

* * *

The one big thing I was praying about was the finances that we would need to keep The Centre up and running once we had guests in. We calculated that we would need around £600–£1,000 each month. We had prayed about this and, like all other areas we were concerned about, we knew that God would provide all the finances required to see this project succeed.

On Tuesday 26 October I wrote in my journal:

Today as I was praying, I realised how Noah must have felt. I'm sure he had a few weak moments and a few doubts about the idea of building an enormous boat in the desert! How was it all going to work out? Had he heard from God? Was it all in his own imagination? Sometimes in my weaker moments I think like that. I don't sleep well at nights. It is all going around in my head when I am trying to get to sleep. It all seems too much for me at times. Then I realise, and remember, that it is not dependent on me. Its success or failure is not up to me. It is God's idea, His project. I am just co-labouring with him to see people healed, delivered, set free and changed for the better. I have to lay it all down before Him and watch what He will do. He will be glorified. He will be honoured. He will be exalted in all the earth.

On Saturday 6th November I had a pleasant surprise. We were at Hazel and Matt's for our grandson's birthday party. Before leaving, they both looked at me and said there was something they wanted to ask me. I wondered what they were going to say. 'Would you do us the honour of being at the birth of our third child at Christmas?' I was flabbergasted. I never, ever thought I would be at the birth of any child but my own! It was such a shock to me. Then Hazel said 'I asked you because it is something that I would want my daughter to ask me.' I nearly cried at that point.

'I would love to!' I said, quickly making my decision. 'I would be honoured to accept.' I came home so excited about the prospect and planned on packing my suitcase as soon as possible!

* * *

We had a good time at the Centre on Sunday 14th November with two other couples. We shared communion together, Norman went around all the rooms blowing a shofar and we prayed and declared words over the place. When everyone left, Geoff sneaked a wodge of £20 notes in my hand. I didn't count them until we got home. When I did, it was £200 altogether. WOW! What a day.

Work on the bathroom/shower room continued. Peter cut a hole in the wall so we could put a door into the shower room. On 18 November Phil drained off the water in the tank so he could remove the radiator in the bathroom. I went off to do some shopping, but when I came back to see how he was getting on the radiator was still firmly attached to the wall! There was water on the floor and a hose pipe attached to one end of the radiator and the other end of the pipe was down the toilet. Horrible black water was coming out! Phil then sawed off the pipes that were attached to the radiator and then quite simply removed it from the wall. I then got a screwdriver and took the brackets off. Hallelujah, job done!

Over the following two days Peter finished putting up the stud partitioning as a dividing wall between the bathroom and the shower room and started fitting the new door on to the shower room. It looked fabulous. Things were beginning to take shape.

Meanwhile we got a good deal at a shop in Peterborough on a shower tray and cubicle so we ordered those. Also a couple from our church delivered another basin and toilet for the shower room. On 22 November Phil and his friend put up the plasterboard on the stud partitioning and checked the soakaway for the shower.

The following day Alan, a friend of ours from church who owns a carpet/floor coverings shop in Market Deeping, came over to measure the bathroom and shower room ready to put new floor covering down for us free of charge! We have to have that non-slip stuff and we chose a lovely mottled colour for both floors.

On Sunday 28 November I wrote in my journal:

> I believe God is teaching me to be patient in this season. It is one of the 'fruit of the Spirit' so I need it! Some things seem to take so long to get done and I can get a little frustrated with it all! God has told

me twice today and once yesterday to be patient. In my daily readings it came up twice and someone said to me on Friday at our Food Hygiene Course that God was teaching me to be patient. I am trying!

The next day I had a text from Mark (our electrician) that said his five-year-old son had got chicken pox so he would not be able to come for the next few days. Then Warners said the plumber, who was supposed to have called three weeks ago about the heating, had been so busy that he couldn't make it. He would come soon! Janice, patience!

The end of November was very cold with below freezing temperatures. Snow prevented some from getting to our Trustees' Meeting. We had a great evening though. We looked at the accounts and the forecast for next year and on paper we had enough money to last us until August! And we were still planning on opening either the beginning of February or March 2011.

The cold weather continued. We prayed we wouldn't have any burst pipes! On Wednesday 1st December I was in the orange room and noticed that the window sill and all around the window frame was wet. Then as I walked around the room, I noticed that my feet were squelching in the brand-new carpet which had been fitted. 'Norman!' I shouted. 'Come and have a look at this.' After some investigation, he concluded it must be a leak from the radiator. He was right. The heating engineer who came later that day said there was a pin missing from the valve and the radiator had probably been leaking for about three weeks. The wetness around the window frame was condensation due to the leak. He got a new pin to stop the leak but said he would come back to replace all five radiator valves at some point.

In the mean time we needed to get the place ready for our 'Open House' the following Friday evening and all day on Saturday.

We borrowed a VAX machine from church which sucked up the water from the soggy carpet. We put the heating on but the boiler kept cutting out (another job for Warners to sort!) so I put a portable heater in the orange room.

On Wednesday it was too cold for John to do the flooring in the bathroom but Mark plastered the stud partitioning in the bathroom/ shower room and put the ceiling light in. Peter H also dropped by and helped to put up a shelf in the laundry room and a towel holder, plus two light fittings in the twin room. And the Salvation Army Officer came with another gentleman to have a look around and asked me if I needed another bed. God is so good. He knew I needed one. It has been such an encouraging day. I feel so incredibly blessed.

On the Thursday evening before our Open House event, we narrowly avoided a disaster.

Norman went to the Healing Rooms at 6pm. Not long after I got a call from him saying there was water coming through the ceiling in the corridor. The carpet was sopping wet and he didn't know quite what to do. I told him where there were some buckets, so he put them down to catch the water which was coming down very quickly now. I immediately phoned Warners and they said someone would be round as soon as they could. I then phoned Amanda and asked her to pray with me that this would not get any worse. I then called Norman and he told me a 22mm copper pipe in the loft had split at a joint and there was a 6-inch pipe-shaped icicle across the gap! We needed to find the stopcock quickly or else the whole lot would cave in. We got to praying very hard at this point and declared that God is the God of the impossible. If He could part the Red Sea then He could stop us from having a catastrophe. I phoned Norman and he told me they had got into the boiler room and there was water under their feet. They had to work quickly to find the leaks and stopcock. Norman also found another wet carpet in the staff bedroom. Thankfully, Mark (our electrician) popped in and he had just the right sized allen key to stop the water leaking from the radiator in there. Given that we still had the VAX machine (thank you Lord), Norman sucked up all the excess water in the carpets and finally came home at 9.45pm.

When he described all the events to me, we both realised that God was in it all and the right people came at the right time to prevent a catastrophe. I wrote in my journal:

The enemy is trying everything he can to stop us from having our 'Open House' tomorrow and Saturday. We have no heating or water but we shall still go ahead. What he thinks will destroy will only show God's great power and glory in this place. I am so excited about this weekend even more than before. I believe something significant is going to happen as the enemy has done all he can to stop this from going ahead.

A few days' later Alison told me what had happened at the Healing Rooms on Thursday evening as the intercessors were praying about the flooding. Alison had the words 'birth pangs' and then 'the waters broke'. She felt we had been going through the pains of childbirth and now it was time to give birth to this project. The burst pipes and leaking radiators were a sign to us and we must take courage from all this and look forward to the opening.

* * *

We had thirty visitors at our Open Day, including six from Nottingham, two from Halifax and a couple from March near Peterborough. One of our visitors was a very well-dressed man in a suit and dickey bow and I realised it was Mr Tickle! Yes, Mr Graham Tickle, the professional pianist who had offered to play for us when we have afternoon tea. He was on his way to play at The George Hotel in Stamford but he stopped by to have a look at the place.

During the day I ferried people backwards and forwards to our house so they could go to the toilet!

Overall, it was a very encouraging day. One visitor offered to replace a tatty old carpet in the rose room free of charge and even got his tape measure from his car and measured the room there and then! Another person offered to do some gardening for us and another some decorating plus others wanted to help in any way they could. God is so good. He is truly an amazing God.

* * *

On Tuesday 14 December we had some bad news. Mark at Warners told me all the work on the central heating had stopped. The system was old. The tank, the boiler and the pipes all needed replacing and it would be very costly to do and it was too risky to mend the radiators at this time. He said that they may have to close the Well Head Centre down. We needed a miracle.

Soon after hearing this, I sent out an URGENT PRAYER REQUEST to all our Prayer Support Team to ask them to stand with us in prayer for this situation. God is much bigger than this. We will see HIS glory and HIS provision over this project.

At our Management Meeting that Friday we discussed the situation and committed everything to God in prayer.

The Lord particularly encouraged us from Isaiah 40 and 41 from the Message version of the Bible. Here are some selected verses:

'Don't panic. I'm with you. There's no need to fear for I'm your God. I'll give you strength. I'll help you. I'll hold you steady, keep a firm grip on you ... I'm transforming you from worm to harrow, from insect to iron. As a sharp-toothed harrow you'll smooth out the mountains, turn those tough old hills into loamy soil. You'll open the rough ground to the weather, to the blast of sun and wind and rain, but you will be confident and exuberant, expansive in The Holy of Israel! The poor and homeless are desperate for water, their tongues parched and no water to be found. I'm there for them, and I, God of Israel, will not leave them thirsty. I'll open up rivers for them on the barren hills, spout fountains in the valleys. I'll turn the baked clay bad lands into a cool pond, the waterless waste into splashing creeks. I'll plant the red cedar in that treeless wasteland, also acacia, myrtle and olive. I'll place the cypress in the desert, with plenty of oaks and pines. Everyone will see this. No one can miss it ... unavoidable, indisputable evidence that I, God, personally did this. It is created and signed by The Holy of Israel.'

Then Amanda had a picture of me being a darning needle with gold thread in it. We are going to be mending people's lives. They will be stronger than they were before.

God is so good. He can move the mountains, but He has also given us the authority to move them in prayer. Mountains of lack, mountains of financial insecurity, mountains of no heating or water. He is an awesome God and we trust Him completely to complete the work He has begun. We are not going to give up or give in. We are overcomers and we shall get the spoils.

More encouragement came in my daily reading from UCB on 20th December. It was entitled 'Life will test you.' There were seven points to it as follows:

1. Being in the will of God requires you to go through storms. 'Many are the afflictions of the righteous, but the LORD delivereth him out of them all' (Psalm 34:19 KJV).

2. When you can't see Him, His eye is still on you. You are never out of His sight, His care or His reach.

3. He will never give you an assignment you cannot complete without His help, so don't try it alone. *(That one really hit me!)*

4. If you let it, fear will cloud your thinking and keep you from recognising Him when He comes to you.

5. First, He will speak to you, then to the circumstances that threaten you. When He does, you'll experience supernatural peace. *(I am waiting for that right now!)*

6. When your boat is in the middle of the storm, the best is yet to come! *(I believe that is where I am right now!)*

7. The darkest hour is just before the dawn. Rejoice! The sun will shine again, God won't fail you. *(Bless God, I know where I am.)*

On 21st December we still had no news about the central heating! However, Peter D came to finish off the door to the shower room and it looked wonderful as if it had always been there! Also, Mark at Warners gave a slightly more positive update on the heating situation. They had had a company round to look at what was needed and they were now waiting for a quote. He said if it wasn't too astronomical, they would get the job done as soon as possible. I asked him if they could section off our bungalow by putting a zone valve in or a stop tap somewhere so all the water doesn't have to go around all the other three bungalows before it reaches ours. He said that they had already been thinking about this and were looking into it. God is so good.

* * *

Another birth was about to take place. On Sunday 27 December Hazel was admitted to hospital as her blood pressure was high so Matt took her in and we looked after their two boys. Whilst there we popped over to see my sister who also lives in Lincoln but our conversation was interrupted by a phone call. 'Hi, Janice. It's Ann. I'm out walking the dog and have just walked past The Centre. I can see water gushing out under the front door.' This was the last thing I needed to hear. I immediately phoned Warners but there was no reply as they were on holiday for Christmas. I couldn't think who else I could contact. No answer from Phil, the plumber but Mark (my electrician) responded. He said he would go round and take a look. A while later he phoned back 'I've managed to stop the water for the time being,' he said. 'I just hope it lasts until Warners get it sorted properly next week.' I phoned Amanda and a few others and asked them to pray.

Meanwhile, there was a slight emergency at the hospital. The staff on duty couldn't hear the baby's heartbeat so Hazel was rushed upstairs to the delivery room. She was put on a heart monitor and also a blood pressure monitor and a drip in her arm. They were very attentive to her. When Matt arrived at 9.00pm that evening he was told that there was nothing doing so he could go home. As she wasn't due until 10 January, they wouldn't do anything to bring the baby on. Anyway at 10.30pm we had a phone call from the hospital asking us to go in.

When Matt and I arrived at the delivery room Hazel was having contractions every three minutes. Her waters had broken and the labour was underway. She was doing really well until the midwife was a little concerned about the baby's heart beat again. She pressed the red alarm button and about six or seven people came charging in to see what they could do to help. I immediately walked out of the room into a little side room and prayed like I had never prayed before, and left Matt there. There were far too many people in there for me! I prayed that God would send an angel into the room. Little did I know that Hazel had prayed the same prayer. Matt came to fetch me when all the panic was over. They had fixed a monitor on top of the baby's head so they could hear the heart beat properly. Hazel was looking at the figures on the machine during the evening/night and was getting a little concerned about what she saw and heard. The midwife reassured her at all times.

At about 11.30pm she had an internal examination. 'Everything is coming along fine,' the midwife said. 'We are just going to have to wait now.'

Two hours later Hazel really wanted to push but the midwife kept telling her not to yet. In the end she fetched the doctor and the doctor told Hazel to push when she had her next contraction as she wanted to fix something else to the baby's head. When Hazel had her next contraction, she pushed so hard that the baby nearly shot off the delivery table! The midwife just managed to put one glove on and grab hold of the baby in time. Then the midwife put the baby onto Hazel. 'It's a boy,' said Matt. 'And he is going to be called Gabriel Joshua.' (Gabriel means God's messenger) I cried. I had been praying for God to send an angel into the room and he did! He weighed in at 5lbs 9oz. Perfectly formed. So beautiful and so small. Hazel was so relieved that it was all over for her. Matt then asked me to cut the umbilical cord. WOW! What an honour that was for me. After that, we all wanted to hold Gabriel so the staff left us in peace for the next two hours. We were all so thrilled that he had been delivered safely through a natural childbirth as they were preparing us all for a caesarean and none of us wanted that. God had it all planned. The timing and everything, was perfect. Our God is an awesome God.

Countdown to OPEN DAY

Your vision will be tried by situations that either make or break you. Bill Gothard describes this process as the birth of the vision, the death of a vision and the resurrection of the vision. When you've no funds, no friends and no fight left in you (the death stage), remember the words of Jesus: 'Unless a grain of wheat falls to the ground and dies, it remains alone, but if it dies (to self) it produces much grain.' John 12:24.

When your vision dies and God resurrects it, you begin to talk and act differently. With ego subtracted and grace added, you start saying with the psalmist 'I had fainted, unless I had believed to see the goodness of the LORD in the land of the living' (Psalm 27:13 KJV).

These were the words I read from my UCB Word For Today (which is a free publication) in early January 2011. There were many instances that year when we had to let go of our vision and allow God to resurrect it.

Following on from the leaks from the radiators at the end of 2010, our first major concern was to get the hot water and heating system fully functioning. But until that happened, we couldn't risk putting the water on. As it was, in early January we found even more damp carpets, damp walls and damp ceilings. We contacted Warners that day to see what was happening with the central heating, little did we know how long the process would take and how many setbacks we would encounter along the way.

On Monday 10th January the local central heating company came back to look at the job and promised to give Warners a quote to repair or replace the radiator valves as soon as they could. On 23 January Mark at Warners told us that the quote had come through and that the work was going to start the following Thursday. However, on 3

February Mark told me that when they turned the water supply back on it burst the boiler in the boiler room, totally destroying it! There was water gushing out under the boiler room doors and into the street, so they had to turn it all off again. Mark said they (Warners) would get a further quote for a new tank and boiler just for our bungalow, meaning that our water system would be independent and not connected to the other three! Now, that was good news to me because we had wanted this to happen from the start.

I emailed all our Prayer Support Team and got them praying that Warners would accept the quote, when it arrived, and get the job done.

At the end of February, we went up to Perth in Scotland to celebrate Les and Pat's fortieth Wedding Anniversary (Les is Norman's brother). We had a lovely time with all the family but early on the Sunday morning Les phoned our hotel room with some distressing news. They had just found Richard, their 38-year-old autistic son dead in his bed. We were both shocked and dazed. We went round later that morning and offered to stay a few days longer but they said there was nothing we could do now. They were just waiting for the autopsy to find out the cause of death and then they would be able to organise the funeral arrangements. So we left on Monday morning as planned.

On our return Mark told me they had received a quote for £12,000 to complete the job and Philip Warner was not willing to pay that amount but had gone back to the heating company to see if there was any way they could bring the price down.

We really needed a breakthrough. We could see the finishing line and we just needed the final push to see this project birthed.

On 11 March we met up with the heating company and Mark at The Centre and the company said they could only reduce the quote by £2,000 which is still far too much to expect Warners to pay, and we have no money! We phoned British Gas and EoN but they said it would cost £2,000 to change the meter for us. Perhaps another heating company could help us, but who? Over the next week we tried a couple of other firms but both said they wouldn't be able to do the job as the gas meter is an industrial one and they aren't registered to work on those. It seemed we had reached a stalemate. But we weren't giving up. That afternoon we met up with Amanda and Alison for an hour of prayer, power and praise. We each brought promises of scripture to declare and a faith-declaring song to sing, and stormed around the house, standing on God's promises.

On the same day I received an email from a church friend:

'He is absolutely delighted with you and all that you are doing. He is there with you. He is in your meetings and He sings and dances with you. When you shout, He shouts. When you praise, He is praising with you. When you sing, He sings. He is so happy. He is delighted at all you are doing. He covers you wherever you go. He is with you. He is saturating your land and the building. His presence is there. He is raising the level. He is pushing back boundaries. He is opening new doors for you and He is delighted with this. They are very good doors. This is a new season. You are on the right path. He is guiding you and helping you. There is going to be provision. He will provide for you. (I have a picture of the Lord sweeping in lots of coins before Him.) He is protecting your land and all that is in it. He is with you and for you. So keep going.'

* * *

By 23rd March we decided we had postponed things long enough and we all agreed that Friday 20 May would be the Opening Day whether or not the heating was working by then. At the same time, we kept praying and believing for a miracle of finances to pay for it.

I wrote in my journal:

Everywhere I look at the moment I see these words 'Rest' … 'The battle is the Lord's' … 'Be anxious for nothing'. I think the Lord is trying to tell me something! We are on the edge. We are ready to give birth and the enemy knows it and he will do all he can to put a stop to it. Well, he is in for a shock. He is a defeated foe. He will not win. We shall overcome. The Lord is our victory banner and He cannot fail. So we march on and conquer.

On Wednesday 6 April in my quiet time the first scripture I opened up was Habakkuk 2:2–3:

> 'Then the Lord answered me and said, "write the vision and make it plain on tablets that he may run who reads it. For the vision is yet for an appointed time, but at the end it will speak and it will not lie. Though it tarries wait for it, because it will surely come, it will not tarry."'

I wrote in my journal:

> This really does encourage me. When I read God's word it is faith-building when things seem to be at a standstill. Faith to keep on keeping on. Keep trusting. Keep believing. Watch and wait seem to be the buzz words for me at the moment.

I didn't have long to wait. That evening Mark at Warners let us know that they had accepted the quote of £10,000 and were going to contact the heating company on Monday to say go ahead with the work. PRAISE GOD! He can do the impossible.

However, there were further delays – the heating company wanted to make sure that the quote would not change once they started the work. They made a check of all the system and pipework in the boiler room and loft but then work stalled when the person who had done the check was off sick.

Our other big headache at this time related to our plumber, Phil. He had been reliable up to this point so it was concerning and frustrating when he didn't respond to our frequent phone messages and texts. We were pleased with the work he'd done so far and had paid him but we needed him to come back to finish the job in the bathroom and shower room. My journal is peppered with the words 'still no plumber' and 'we're waiting for the plumber again!' Three months went by with no response from him. On 22 March I decided to try his number one last time and he actually answered his phone: 'I was thinking of coming over tomorrow to finish off the job,' he said. I nearly fell off my chair!

He came the following day and started the pipe work in the bathroom. He said that he had got a new phone and he couldn't get on with it which may be why he hadn't answered any of my calls! But, having promised to come the following week to finish off, we heard nothing from him. On 5th April, I wrote:

Still we wait for Phil, the plumber to come! We seem to have lost all contact with him again! The Lord is really teaching me a valuable lesson in all of this. I am learning to be more patient, more tolerant and more at peace in every difficult and trying situation. I am learning to WATCH, WAIT and BELIEVE that God will do all He has promised He would.

By the end of the month, I made the decision to contact another plumber to see if he would come and look at the job which needed to be done in the shower room and the bathroom.

* * *

Despite the ongoing saga with the heating company and the plumber, we made good progress in other areas of the project. Lots of people gave their time, resources and skills which was a real blessing. During January Gavin decorated the last bedroom and put a second coat of emulsion in the lilac room. Peter K painted the shower room ceiling and door frames and wrestled with putting new locks on some of the bedroom doors. Phil the plumber put loads of pipework in the shower room and bathroom.

In February Peter D fireproofed all the bedroom doors and Ian did some more tiling in the shower room and the kitchen, which looks fab! Peter H put a mirror up in one of the bedrooms, a very large heavy cupboard in the laundry room and all the fire extinguishers on the appropriate walls. Mark (our electrician/plasterer) plastered the wall separating the bathroom from the shower room but it took a long time to dry as there was no heating. They had a great time of fellowship with each other as they were doing their different jobs! It was encouraging to see.

Also, during the early part of the year all our volunteers completed a couple more courses: Fire Safety and Risk Assessment. After the day's teaching at the Fire Safety Course, we had fun trying out fire extinguishers. I was surprised how light it was and how easy it was to pull the trigger!

While others were making progress at the bungalow, we continued to acquire items to go in it. In January we picked up a large hamper from Bourne Textile Services. They supplied us with twenty of everything free of charge – bath towels, hand towels, duvet covers, bottom sheets, pillow cases and four large table cloths too. Earlier in the month I had met Mickey, a guy at our church who owns a business that embroiders logos onto fabrics. He was very excited about our project and said he would love to design and print the logos free of charge! So, in February we took all our towels, pillowcases, duvet covers and sheets over to his factory and had The Well Head Centre logo printed on them. They looked really beautiful and very classy.

We also had to sort out the items on the list the Fire Service had given us to make the whole place fireproof. Mark, our electrician, told me it would cost around £1000 to get all he needed to achieve this. We hadn't budgeted for any of it but we started to pray about it. On 14th January I received a letter from the Fire Service letting me know that they wanted to do an audit of the building on 8 March so I phoned Mark, our electrician, to find out when he could make a start.

'I'll come next week,' he said. 'And, by the way, I've been rummaging around in my garage. I've got a zone box which I was given a few years ago. We could use that if it still works. That will save you £200. Then I've got some fire cable left over from another job which I could use to finish off all the cabling in the loft. Oh, and I've found a few spare smoke detectors as well.'

I started laughing. 'You seem to have accumulated a lot of stuff in your garage, Mark!'

'Yes, well I don't like to throw anything away. You never know when it may come in handy.' Mark saved us £1000 as most of what he needed was lying around in his garage!

In the end, following on from the Fire Inspection Mark told me the cost of doing all the electrical work needed to make the place safe in case of a fire would be around £350. We really didn't have any choice in the matter. I told him to just go ahead and get all the equipment and materials he needed to get the job done and God would supply.

* * *

And God did continue to provide financially for all our needs – a cheque for £120 in January; £500 from the Healing Rooms team from Nottingham when they came to visit, a cheque for £1,000 from a friend plus £100 from my nephew Alan in March plus a cheque from the Insurance company to help pay for the water bill we had following all those leaks over Christmas. On 3rd April I was given a lovely surprise package containing 250 printed letterheads and 250 'with compliments' slips from David & Gill. In May alone we received over £3,000 in gifts and donations which meant we could stay open for at least the next six months. Praise God.

We also added to our list of referrers: a couple, both GPs, that Amanda bumped into and a Parish Nurse from Uppingham, near Stamford who came to visit the Centre.

God was bringing the right people to us and this included prayer supporters. Every month I sent out prayer pointers by email and post to all those who wanted to be part of this ministry. We knew we wouldn't function properly without this and had many faithful prayers.

* * *

On Thursday 7 April I was shocked and stunned to hear that one of our faithful Healing Rooms team members and also a volunteer at The Well Head Centre has been told that she only has between two and three months to live. She has got secondary cancer. Amanda is taking her and another member of our team away to a retreat that is specifically available for those going through cancer treatment. We prayed God would do a miracle in both of their lives while they are there.

* * *

A week later I had a very exciting delivery from the postman – 500 newly printed, fresh off the press, Well Head Centre leaflets. They looked fabulous! Our family helped to fold them and by 23rd April I had sent out all the invitations to our Opening Day Celebrations.

That day I wrote in my journal:

In my reading today I was really encouraged. It was all about 'Standing Firm' and not giving up. That He is with me in the 'Centre of the Storm' and that sometimes it takes time for God to answer our prayers because He is working on every aspect of it to bring it into fulfilment. It doesn't matter how much I worry or get stressed it is not going to make things happen any quicker! I am still learning to trust and wait on God.

However, towards the end of April things seemed to be at a standstill. People seemed to be backing off but there was still a lot to do before 20 May and I felt a little overwhelmed by it all. I started to wonder if I had got things wrong. Had I taken a wrong turning somewhere along the way? Had I gone off ahead of God? I felt alone and vulnerable.

On Friday 29 April I got up early as I felt I needed to get alone with God and seek His face and His will. I started singing 'Our God is greater' and it made me realise God is in charge. He would work it all out and we would see this come to fruition.

On the Saturday Norman and I went shopping in Spalding and bought a watering can, brushes, bins and photo frames for all our certificates and fire safety notices for all the bedrooms. While we were there, we had a freshly made apple juice at one of the churches. The apples were put into a crusher whole, and out came a beautiful, green drink – I had never tasted anything like it before. That evening during our Bible study and prayer time we read John 16:29-33. We stopped at verse 33 for a while looking at the word 'tribulation.' In my Bible there is a section at the bottom of the page called 'word wealth.' It explains words in much more detail. We decided to read what it said about tribulation:

> *'Pressure, oppression, stress, anguish, adversity, affliction, crushing, squashing, squeezing, distress. That's putting a lot of pressure on that which is free and unfettered. It is like a spiritual bench-pressing. The word is used of crushing grapes or olives in a press.'*

I said to Norman, 'That's how I feel right now.' Then we understood that we should expect tribulation but only good would come out of it. Just like that apple juice being crushed brought out all the flavour, so our being crushed would result in something even more powerful.

On Monday 2 May, God spoke to me again in a surprising way. When I walked into the dining room to have my prayer time, I noticed something different about my cactus plant on the windowsill. I saw what seemed to be a very small yellow flower appearing on the top of it. I had had this cactus for about ten years and it had never flowered before! I felt God was showing me how sometimes things can look as if nothing is happening and all is in vain, but we just need to be patient, watch and wait to see what God will do. His timing is always perfect.

The evening of 4th May it was all hands to the pump when our Life Group came and helped. We needed a very large hole digging in the quad area between the bungalow and a manhole chamber to fit waste pipes in. Phil, one of our life group members volunteered to dig the hole. When he had done it we could hardly see him! He is only short in stature and he looked so funny down this enormous hole that looked like a grave.

David and Gill cleaned all the windows for us, inside and out. Sue and Phil (another Phil) dusted some rooms. Norman emulsioned the ceiling in the bathroom and then did some vacuuming. I painted the bottom 10 inches of the door black, varnished the window frame and then ironed and put up the curtains in the lilac room.

I tell you, the smell in the lilac room is amazing. It smells lovely and clean and fresh. We have had some weird and disgusting smells in the bungalow since we took it over, but now we have some gorgeous smells creeping through. It looks fabulous when you open that bedroom door now. It is my favourite! It is all beginning to look like a home should look. We are getting there.

On 5th May we had just fifteen days to go before our Opening Day. I decided to record these as a countdown in my journal:

Thursday 5 May 15 DAYS TO GO

The carpet fitter fitted the carpet in the orange room which looks fabulous. I planted some double petunias at the front door and sorted all the bedroom door keys out and put them on key fobs with the corresponding colours to the rooms. We have white, lilac, orange, blue, rose and yellow – the colours of the tins of paint Branch Bros gave us at the very beginning.

Friday 6 May 14 DAYS TO GO

Some of the Healing Rooms team went to the annual Healing Rooms Conference in Halifax. We had a great time together and were totally amazed to receive half the weekend's offering for the Well Head Centre! God is so good.

Saturday 7 May 13 DAYS TO GO

We made quite a lot of good contacts at the conference and gave out lots of our leaflets. Whilst there I fell in love with a painting called 'Breakthrough'; it was gorgeous. It was £45 but worth every penny. The lady didn't take cards as payment so I was just wondering how I might pay for it when a lady from Nottingham Healing Rooms came up to me and said that she wanted to buy it for The Well Head Centre. I just burst into tears. I gave her a big hug and left her to pay! God is so good.

Sunday 8 May 12 DAYS TO GO

Our last day at the conference in Halifax. When Amanda met us all in the hotel reception area as we were waiting to go in for breakfast she said, 'Happy Birthday' instead of 'Good Morning.' We said 'It isn't any of our birthdays today, Amanda.' But she said 'It's prophetic.' We were giving birth and we were going to receive gifts like at a party. Well during the day we received two more monetary gifts.

Monday 9 May 11 DAYS TO GO

I am still waiting for a call from Mark at Warners to let me know that the heating system is being replaced and will be up and running for 20 May. And I'm waiting for the plumber to let me know when he can plumb the bath in. Ian, our tiler can't do the tiling until the flooring and bath have been done. Amanda and Carol came over this evening to help clean up the place. Carol cleaned all the glass in the corridor. Amanda steamed all the carpets. Norman put up all the Fire Evacuation signs in all the bedrooms and the office. It all smells so much sweeter now when you walk in.

Tuesday 10 May 10 DAYS TO GO

'You only have the best, don't you? I can see you're a perfectionist!' said Philip (Warner) after we'd given him a tour of the centre. 'And it looks more like a home than an institution.' This was good to hear and that we could use his car park on our Opening Day if we needed to. Other visitors that day included Tom (one of the Healing Rooms team) who weeded the driveway. Then Margaret and Brian, who are part of the WOW Team at church came to see how we could give The Centre a WOW factor for the Opening Day. Also, two young men, both called Peter, finished off the flooring in the bathroom and shower room.

I realised today that I had miscalculated how many wicker chairs I needed for all the bedrooms because I'd forgotten to include one extra for the twin room and two for the staff bedroom. Well, this morning during my prayer time I told the Lord that I had miscalculated and so I asked Him for three more! While we were having our Trustees Meeting in the evening, one of our Trustees called Steve received a text message from a friend who said he had three wicker chairs he wanted to get rid of and did he know of anyone who might need them? Steve didn't know what I had requested in prayer that morning! Our God is so good. He loves us to be specific in prayer.

After our Trustees Meeting three people from the Baptist Church in Bourne came to help with a few jobs. They unpacked our new tumble dryer which was donated by The Salvation Army in Bourne. They set up our two second-hand washing machines in the laundry room. They took up all the dust sheets and vacuumed the carpets and washed all the basins in the bungalow. And they assembled a bed and a set of drawers and put them in the lilac room.

Wednesday 11 May 9 DAYS TO GO

Norman and I went to The Centre tonight at around 6.00pm and started painting. Norman did the bathroom walls and I undercoated the radiator. Then I did some vacuuming in the bedrooms. We were just planning to leave when a lady from the Baptist Church came to see if there was anything she could do to help. She helped us move some beds around and then we started to take all the protective covers off all the new mattresses which had been donated by Fitzgerald's Beds in Bourne. Then Mark came to continue getting all the lights working in the bedrooms. We finally all left at around 9.50pm. We had a great time together. It is all beginning to take shape and the fusty smell seems to have all but gone now!

Thursday 12 May 8 DAYS TO GO

Norman and I were planning on staying in today but the plumber rang and said he wanted to come over and plumb in the bath. He did a great job. The bath (which Brent Warner provided for us) looks lovely. He didn't fully complete the job as there was a piece missing from one of the pipes and the bath panel was split.

We can now at least get the tiler in to tile the bathroom and do the emulsioning. It is coming on. The plumber is coming back one day next week to plumb the toilet and basin in and complete the shower in the shower room. Mark also came in the evening to check we had lights in every room. He is now going to carry on with all the fire safety regulations.

Josh has finished our website and it is fab. It gives the countdown days, hours, minutes and seconds to our opening! Josh will let us have the statistics of how many people click on our website monthly. That will be interesting reading.

Friday 13 May 7 DAYS TO GO

Norman and I spent the whole day preparing for Saturday's Volunteer Induction Day. It all seemed to go very well. The tiler came to do the bathroom and Mark and Gill came to do some stuff. Norman and I went off to Spalding at around 4.30pm to do a bit of shopping for The Centre. We ended up at Sheddies Fish and Chip Shop n Spalding for our favourite fish and chips meal.

Sunday 15 May 5 DAYS TO GO

After church today Norman and I went out for lunch with two of our special friends. Then we went straight over to Lincoln to visit our daughter, son-in-law and three lovely grandchildren. We also picked up a mattress and a lock for the office from my brother Geoff who is a locksmith.

Monday 16 May 4 DAYS TO GO

Before we left Lincoln, we went to get some things for The Centre like mirrors, toilet seats, waste bins for the bedrooms, door handles etc. On our way back we did a detour and ended up in Peterborough to have our final Management Meeting with Amanda to make sure everything was ready for the opening on Friday. We eventually arrived back home totally exhausted but excited.

Tuesday 17 May 3 DAYS TO GO

We were at The Well Head Centre all day today painting, cleaning and clearing out some more stuff. Peter, Peter and Ian came and were faithfully doing whatever needed to be done. We now have a lock on the office door. The gardens are looking better too. We still have a grave-like hole in the quad area ready for the plumber so we shall probably have to conceal that area for Friday! We don't want any accidents. We went to get four new rose bushes and two clematis plants for the front garden. Then I went to get seven photo frames for the certificates which will then go on the walls. I bought one more tin of magnolia emulsion for the bathroom as we had run out. We are both quite exhausted and there is still lots more to do. To add to the stress, I have an error on my emails and so it is not sending them out. I will contact our son Glyn in the morning and see if he can sort it for me.

Wednesday 18 May 2 DAYS TO GO

Over the last three days I have been reading about Elijah. Sometimes when the going gets tough I love to read how others coped with their stress but stayed focused on their task. Elijah was feeling quite dry and helpless not knowing what to do next with the situation he found himself in. Elijah had to discount all the 'no rain' reports he kept on getting. The account of Elijah is in I Kings 18:41-44.

When you know God has promised you something you must tune out the negativity around you. Stand on His Word and keep believing. What He says to you will be more real than anything that's happening in your circumstances. But be warned: what you hear in your spirit may go against what you hear in your intellect, or what you have in your bank, or what's happening at work, or what's taking place at home, or what's happening in your body. There was nothing happening in the natural.

Finally, you must position yourself to receive. Elijah put his face between his knees. That's the birthing position! Today what you sense within you is real, but if you don't get into position and push, it won't happen. If you do, God will bless you with abundance.

Every success begins with somebody taking a small step or sowing a small seed which usually represents all they have at that moment in time. Simply stated: everything big starts with something small. If you are not willing to start small, you can't start at all.

The servant who kept telling Elijah nothing was happening, finally saw something. It was just a tiny cloud, but it had great potential. God loves to use things that we think are insignificant. When God promises you something, He doesn't need anything big to make it happen.

That really encourages me to keep on keeping on. He will do all that needs to be done if I stay faithful and committed to Him and His plans for The Well Head Centre.

Thursday 19 May 1 DAY TO GO

We hadn't heard from the plumber so I thought I had better phone him to see if he was planning to come today. He didn't answer his phone. I tried him later in the day but he still didn't answer. We were getting a bit concerned. The toilet wasn't connected. The basin and pedestal were both lying on the shower room floor. The shower wasn't connected and it would look awful for tomorrow if things didn't change.

The WOW Team from our church turned up at 10.30am to make the Centre look stunning and they did not disappoint. They put a VERY LARGE white 'LOVE' sign above our front door which had a white dove at the side of it too. We have beautiful blue and gold material flowing down the wooden uprights which support the canopy over our front door where we shall stand to cut the ribbon tomorrow. They also put a lovely water feature just outside the front door. There is a large display of flowers just as you walk in the building and a jug of flowers on the reception desk. They have arranged flowers in every room. It smells and looks amazing. All the bedrooms look amazing too. There are hearts all over the place and LOVE all over the place too!

I finally had a call from the plumber He is arriving at 4.00pm.

I went to buy some more plants and to get a bag of sand to put in a bucket for those who want to smoke!

The plumber tried to make the shower room look like it was a working shower room but it wasn't. Nothing was connected but at least people will get an idea of what it will look like when it is finished. We can't finish it off until we get some water flowing through!

We have two large blue/grey screens in the garden covering the grave-like hole and the pile of sand and soil that came out of the hole. It does look better now it is all covered!

Peter came to mow the lawns for us today and to put up another screen in the garden to hide the eyesore of the bungalows next door which are still boarded up and look in a terrible state. He made a trellis in the shape of a cross and I will put a couple of clematis there which will grow and look beautiful in the months to come. Mark came round in the evening to finish off some things and Norman trimmed the edges of the lawns. I stayed at home this evening so I could get the programme done for tomorrow. I am shattered! I haven't been sleeping well lately, as you can probably imagine! I have been waking up at around 3.30am each morning and not being able to get back to sleep again. I know it will all calm down after the opening.

Norman arrived home around 10.00pm tonight after being at The Centre all day. Mark got an electric shock whilst doing the electrics and blew a few lights!

I had an email today from Graham Tickle (our afternoon tea pianist) asking us if we would like some music whilst guests were having their refreshments tomorrow? We thought that would be a great idea so I emailed him back and accepted his kind offer.

Friday 20 May The Opening Day

We had a wonderful afternoon together. We started on the front lawn with drinks and chatting to guests. The weather was glorious. There were about thirty people, including distinguished guests, who came to help us celebrate the opening of The Well Head Centre. They included the former Mayor of Bourne Councillor Pet Moisey, who had only just retired that month, together with her husband David; the Volunteer Trainer; Salvation Army Officers, Richard and Heather Durrant; Pastor of the Baptist church,

Andy Warner; Jim Thody from KingsGate Community Church; Graham Tickle our pianist and many other lovely friends and volunteers who just wanted to be there to share in our special day. The photographer from the Bourne Local and the Stamford Mercury took photos of the ceremonial cutting of the ribbon. After the ceremony we all shared in the refreshment and chatted about how it all came into being and all that God had done.

When it was all over, we started to get the rooms ready for the Evening Celebration. We had invited Godfrey Birtill to lead us in an evening of praise and thanksgiving. This being around seven months since his previous visit to lead us in an evening of Celebration, Dedication and Thanksgiving. Once everything was in place, eight of us went into town and shared a meal together at The Nags Head. Then we came back ready to welcome people at 6.30pm.

We had a great time of praise and thanksgiving with Godfrey. We had so many cakes made for us that there were twelve baskets left over! Quite a few guests were unable to make the Opening Day so many people were able to take a selection home with them!

Everyone was thrilled with how The Centre looked and many were offering ways in which they might help. We were very encouraged by all the enthusiasm and support. We got home round 10.00pm. Exhausted, but happy.

For several years this day has been my vision 'only', but now it has become a reality. Praise God!

The floor plan of the bungalow

With the Open Day under our belt, our next goal was to have The Well Centre ready for our guests to start arriving at the beginning of June. As ever, our main concern was when the heating company were going to start work. And, more importantly, would they complete it in time?

On 26th May Warners told us the heating company were ordering a new metal door for the front of the boiler room which would take about two weeks to come. Once that had arrived, they would be around to fit it and the work would begin. As the bungalows next door had been burgled three weeks ago and all the copper piping was removed from the roof, they didn't want the same thing happening again. I could understand this but it meant more waiting. At the end of May, the news was that the doors would be fitted on 12th June and the heating company would come the week after to do all that was necessary to provide heating and water for us. This pushed on the date for guests to come to July.

The heating company arrived on Tuesday 21st June to make a start on the heating system and said they would complete everything by the following Tuesday, 28th June. But then they failed to show up the next morning, and didn't arrive on Thursday until the afternoon. On the 27th everything that could go wrong did go wrong and on the 28th they had found quite a few leaks in the roof. They left with the words 'We'll come back and fix those tomorrow'. My journal entry expresses something of my frustration at this:

> I seem to hear the word 'tomorrow' quite a lot where workmen are concerned! It seems to be the 'buzz' word – there's always tomorrow!

* * *

It seemed as if the closer we got to our goal, the more setbacks we seemed to have – dead mice in the loft, a burglary at the bungalows next to ours and a virus on my computer. Thankfully I knew a rat man who could sort out the rodent problem and our son, Glyn, was able to restore all the files I thought I'd lost on the computer. But the situation with the boiler was another matter:

Wednesday 29 June: I am trying to have the patience I need to cope with the delays but sometimes it does seem to get the better of me. I feel down, weary and forlorn at the moment. I'm sure it will pass.

Thursday 30 June: It has taken me all morning to put all my contacts back on the computer. My head and neck hurt! When I got to The Centre, I found leaky ceilings and buckets of water and wet soggy carpets. The fire room had water dripping through the ceiling light and there was a bucket catching the drips. The carpet was completely soggy too. Two radiators and two basins in the bedrooms were leaking. What a sight! The guys from the heating company had to turn the water off before they went home and are supposed to be coming back tomorrow (that word again!) and Saturday to finish everything off. We have cancelled our 'sleep-over' as there is too much mess around and Mark hasn't finished the fire alarm system. We shall not be opening to guests on 4 July. We have now moved the date to 11 July.

Friday 1 July: Today we only had the electrician from the heating company in to do some work. The plumber was at college. So the work wasn't finished! He said he would come Saturday or Sunday. Even as I am typing all this up, I can feel the stress in my shoulders and neck again. I am typing at such a speed now as I want to see this completed!

Saturday 2 July: No one came.

I'll come back tomorrow

'It's not as bad as it looks,' the heating engineer said as we surveyed the damage on Monday 4th July.

It looked bad enough to me. There were leaks in the ceilings, the corridor and the waiting room. There was water coming through the light fittings and buckets all over the floors. We borrowed a VAX machine from church to help suck up all the water and then gave the carpets a good shampoo ready for Healing Rooms on Tuesday.

The following day we had a chat with the heating company and they told us how all the heating and hot water system would work. They also said they were not here to fix all the radiators that didn't work, only to put a new boiler in the boiler room and fix the leaks in the loft! It was good to have hot water coming through the taps but we needed to sort the radiators out before the winter. The radiators hadn't been used for many years and some of them were corroded and may never work!

When I told Mark that some of the radiators still weren't working, he told me to go around the bungalow and check them all and to make a list of all the problems we had. When I checked there was no heat coming from any of the radiators.

The heating company came back on the Thursday to (as they call it) 'Commission' the boiler. That means to fill in all the paperwork, do all the figures and make sure everything is functioning correctly. In other words, job done. I then sign the paper work, they leave and everyone is happy! So we put the heating on to check all the radiators. We found we still had six that didn't work. We had water coming through the taps, once we had bled them all. It was a horrible dirty colour to begin with but then became lovely and clear. Taps on three of the basins didn't work. Julian (another plumber) arrived today and said that we probably needed new thermal mixing valves and he would put them on for us. He then finished the pipes in the gully outside and put the water back on. He found that we had a leak within the stud partition in between the bathroom and the shower room. He had to take off six tiles and the plasterboard to get to the pipe work. Then he had to find out where the pipe was that was leaking. I said 'You will have to find it. We can't leave it, and besides we have loads of tiles; we can easily replace them!' So he made an even bigger hole in the wall until he found the place where it was leaking and fixed the leak. He then fitted a new thermal mixing valve on the bath so that the water doesn't get too hot. Mark said he would get a quote from a local heating company to repair all our faulty radiators.

* * *

Although the issue with the heating was pending, we started to tick off some of the other larger jobs during July. Mark (our electrician) finished installing all the fire alarm system and by the end of it we had alarms and smoke detectors in every room and a certificate to prove the work had been done. Peter K and Norman assembled the shower cubicle and Peter H came and filled in the very large hole in the quad area where the sewage pipes went and then put the slabs back into place.

With the help of many volunteers, we focused on the finishing touches. The former town Mayor's husband cleaned all twenty-five windows plus five doors. He did a great job!

Other volunteers cleaned out some of the cupboards in the kitchen and laundry room and one of them even tackled the storeroom. We switched the large freezer on as we had received our first supply of freshly baked bread. God's rich supply was coming in!

Some good friends of ours gave us loads of plants and shrubs which we planted, a bookcase and pool table arrived for the lounge and we put some more pictures up. I put a little square colour co-ordinated plaque on all of the bedroom doors so people would know which room was theirs. This colour would also correspond with their key fob.

We also did some induction training with the volunteers. We worked out how to use the cooker and were trained in using the fire alarm system and what all the keys were for on the key fob. Everyone was ready and raring to go.

On Monday 18 July we were officially ready to receive guests into the Centre. To mark the occasion five civic dignitaries visited: the Mayor of the City of Lincoln and her Consort, the Sheriff of the City of Lincoln and the Sheriff's Lady, and the newly appointed Mayor of Bourne. We also had volunteers and Trustees around the place to make everyone feel welcome. They absolutely loved the place.

* * *

Ever since we started this project I had been contacting many funding bodies to try and get some finances coming in. Friends kept telling me to apply to this person and that person. I spent many hours filling in forms. Every application was rejected. All I wanted was to know that we had enough finances for the next six months. It was making me ill. I prayed and told God that I couldn't do this anymore. I believe I saw Him rubbing His hands together and saying to me, 'I have been waiting for you to say this Janice. Now watch what I will do.'

On 11th July I received an email from one of my friend's sons who works for an organisation called Network Peterborough who give out money/grants to Christian organisations who work together with other denominations. He had heard about us from his mother. All we had to do was fill in a short application form and he would do the rest. If we met the criteria we could get anything up to £5,000. I wasn't holding out much hope as I had been rejected on every other request, but my friend told me this would be easy and different. So I quickly filled in the form, waited and prayed.

Four days later I had a phone call. 'Hello, Janice. My name's Tony from Network Peterborough. I wanted to speak to you in person rather than just phone you however, just to say we have considered your application for the grant and we would like to give you the full amount of £5,000.' I was so thrilled. I wrote in my journal:

What a wonderful surprise and a wonderful day. God is so good. We now have the finances to stay open for much longer than six months! Our God is a God of more than enough.

We were constantly surprised and delighted by God's provision. During November I spent many hours looking at new cookers on the internet as the one we had at the time was the one left in the bungalow when we took it over. It was not good! A very good friend at church asked me if we needed anything at The Well Head Centre. 'Well,' I said. 'We are looking for a new cooker at the moment' (thinking he wasn't meaning to buy something so expensive!) But he said, 'You get it and I will pay for it.' I was so shocked at his response. God is so good. We chose a Black Belling electric cooker and Mark (our electrician) came to connect it. It looked so much better than the old one! We were also given a larder fridge, a washing machine, an open plan shelving unit and office equipment that year.

Donations continued to come in steadily, ranging from £20 to £1000 and we added more people to our referrers list including two Macmillan Nurses, one in Sleaford and the other in Grantham, one of the pastors at our church and a GP from our church.

Norman and I drafted an A5 flyer ready to give to our referrers so they could pass the information on to any guests who would be coming to stay with us in The Well Head Centre. We remembered our church had offered to do any printing for us so we sent a copy of the flyer to Simon and the following day he emailed to say they were ready for collection. They were lovely – exactly what we had ordered.

* * *

We continued to have plumbing issues. We found water on the floor in the shower room and when we tried the second-hand washing machines the water was not running through the pipes. The plumber came two weeks later. He found where the leak was coming from and fixed it. He just turned all the valves on at the back then we had water! Simple!

What was less simple to understand was why we still hadn't got any guests coming in. All through August and September I waited for the phone to ring. But there was nothing and I began to feel a bit downhearted and discouraged:

Thursday 22 September: As I was having my prayer time this morning I was reading from a book called Streams in the Desert. It was saying that faith must be tested and the sense of feeling deserted is 'the furnace heated seven times hotter than usual' into which it may be thrown. Blessed is the person who endures such an ordeal. Well, I feel pretty deserted right now. I keep waiting and waiting but nothing (visible) seems to be happening. We are now in September and we had our opening in May. What is happening? I will keep on pressing in. Not giving up. Not looking for signs but trusting in God my Father. He knows the day and it will be the right time.

Friday 23 September: STILL WAITING

Monday 26 September: STILL WAITING

Tuesday 27 September

As I read my UCB (United Christian Broadcasters) daily reading today, I was really encouraged. It was entitled 'God will fulfil His Promise.' I was reminded about Abraham and Sarah in the Bible. They wanted a child but Abraham was, in the natural, too old! The lesson, it read, between praying for a miracle and receiving it is that we will be tested. We will grow and we will learn to trust God more than ever we thought possible. Plus it said when we share our experiences with others don't just tell them how we started on the journey or even where we are today, instead tell them what God has brought us through.

The struggles that we experienced will help others who may be going through similar times right now. Tell them how our faith was tried in the furnace of affliction before we came forth as gold. Sarah spent a terrifying night in a place called 'Gerar' which means 'the halting place'. Yes there will be times when we feel our lives have come to a screeching halt and we are getting nowhere. At these times we need to know that God will be faithful to us. Not only will He bring us through but, like Sarah, our joy will return as we watch Him fulfil His promise to us. WOW! This reading really spoke to me today. I believe this is God letting me know that He hasn't forgotten me. He is still on my case and He will bring it all into fulfilment. His promises are all Yes and Amen.

Today has been a really special day for me. As I was driving down the driveway beside the bungalow this morning guess what, yes you've got it, the Well Head Centre mobile phone rang. I quickly parked up and answered it. It was a pastor from a church in Peterborough. He wanted to chat to me about a couple in his church who he thought would really benefit from spending a few days in The Well Head Centre. He is not at present one of our referrers but it sounds as if he would like to be. I chatted with him and got all his details so I can now send him our Referral Criteria. I will now wait for him to get back to me with a referral. I was so excited to receive this call. I now truly believe the door is open and the guests will start to come in and enjoy all that God has planned for them.

On Saturday 1st October we decided to have a sleepover at The Well Head Centre. We invited Mark our electrician and his wife, David and Gill (two of our Trustees) and Amanda, Natalie and Carol (three of our friends and volunteers). We had a great time. In the morning over breakfast we discussed things that needed slight attention such as the shaver light in the staff bedroom didn't work; the extractor fans in the bathroom and shower rooms stayed on permanently; the heating system hummed all through the night. We all agreed the beds were very comfortable but decided that they should have protective covers on the pillows and mattresses.

The bigger problem, though, was that the carpet in the lounge had an awful smell to it! We had known about it for a while but had not really been able to afford to get a new one as the lounge is very large. I had shampooed it twice and put 'Shake n Vac' on it too but the odour continued to linger. Amanda and Norman both said we should get a new carpet and we planned to have a word with our friend who did the bathroom and shower room floors for us.

The next day Amanda told me she had bumped into that very person and he said to let him have the measurements of the lounge.

A few weeks later our small group from church joined us at The Centre to take up the horrible, smelly carpet ready for the new carpet to be fitted. A man from the carpet company brought us a machine to help us get the carpet up as it was totally stuck to the floor – UUGH! Norman and I started taking out all the furniture before everyone arrived. We were itching to have a go with the machine but first we had to score down the carpet at about 8-inch intervals with a Stanley knife. Norman got the machine ready and I was in position to pull the carpet up once it had all been loosened. Well – we did a little! Then we tried again and did a little more. This was not going to be easy! Then Phil arrived (the one who dug the hole in the garden). He had a go. He also brought a tool similar to the electric one but a manual type. He started pushing and shoving the carpet to get it to come up. Then David and Gill came. David and Phil then got into a sort of a routine and were lifting it up a bit more easily. Then the machine stopped working. We had broken it, I think! We had to leave it and Phil and David carried on with sheer muscle power and determination while Norman scored the carpet so it came up in narrow strips. Sue, from church, went around with a scraper picking up all the little bits left behind. Gill and I got some refreshment ready for the workers.

But the smell had been disturbed! It was awful. It had probably been there for years. It even got into our clothing and we had to throw some away. We got four buckets and mops and I put a concoction of disinfectant, bleach, Jeyes fluid and Flash in the boiling water ready to wash the concrete floor. Since then I've been taught about health and safety and I realise it wasn't a good idea to mix all those liquids together! Mind you, it did get rid of the awful smell!

Two days later the new carpet was all fitted and it looked, felt and smelt wonderful. And it turned out we hadn't broken the machine that helped lift the carpet – we had just tripped the fuse.

* * *

The heating company were slow to come back to us about sorting out the radiators. They made a brief appearance in September and then said they would come back in October to try and fix the problem!

On 6 October I got up early and arrived at The Centre for 8.30am to meet the heating engineer. I had turned the central heating on ready for him so he wouldn't have to wait for it all to heat up. At 9.00am I decided to give him a call. He said 'I have got you down for tomorrow, not today.' That famous buzz word again – 'tomorrow'. I nearly screamed! We had been waiting for two years to get this heating situation sorted so to wait yet another day was more than I could bear. Anyway, as there was nothing more I could do I just said, 'OK, see you tomorrow.'

The next day I went through the same routine and got to the Centre at 8.20am. At 9.00am there was no sign of anyone and I was getting a bit anxious but he arrived shortly after. He looked at all the radiators that weren't working. He took the front casing off them and they were very old and rusty, then he started banging parts of them with some large iron tool! The whole system seemed to shake but one by one they began to get warm. It's amazing what brute force and ignorance can do! When he had finished, only three radiators weren't working. They were all in a bad condition – a miracle any of them worked really. I decided to pray over them and, thank God, two of them then decided to work. I told him that I had prayed over them. He looked at me and said with a smile 'With your prayers and my expertise we have got these radiators working, agreed?' I said, 'Yes, OK!' We finally had heating and hot water and it felt good.

On Monday 10 October we had our first guest! Everything was ready for their arrival – flowers in each room, sweets on the bedside tables and everywhere vacuumed and dusted.

Guests are able to arrive any time after 2.00pm. We were so relieved when we saw her come up the driveway at 5.00pm. So many different thoughts had gone through our minds but they all evaporated as soon as she walked through those front doors. We were so pleased the day had finally arrived when we were welcoming our first guest into The Well Head Centre. Norman made her a cup of coffee and then I took her around The Centre to let her choose which room she would like. She chose the 'Rose' room. I left her there to settle in and read the 'Welcome Pack' and told her to come out when she was ready.

David and Gill came at 6.15pm to take over from us and then Amanda and Carol came at around 8.30pm to do the night-shift.

The following morning I went round to The Centre at about 8.15am to relieve Amanda as she had to go to work. As I drove onto the carpark, I noticed that a window and door of Warner's caravan were wide open. I went over to investigate and to see if anyone was there. I shouted inside but no-one answered. I then realised that it had been broken into during the night. I called Warners immediately and told them what I saw. There was quite a bit of activity during the day as a result with police around all day. We were so pleased that the two cars also on the carpark hadn't been touched and no one in The Centre had heard anything during the night.

Our guest had a good couple of days. She went for a walk, had a free massage from one of our professional volunteers (which she really enjoyed), read a lot and just appreciated the peace in the place. She left some positive feedback on the questionnaire sheet which encouraged us greatly. And to top it off that weekend we received the email we had been waiting for:

We are now a Registered Charity and our number is 1144216. Praise God! We have finally done it. Today I printed this information on all our stationery. I really enjoyed doing that.

The next guests – a couple – came in early November. They enjoyed a beautiful massage and we had a lovely time sharing with them. They wrote in their feedback that they had found time to make major decisions whilst with us.

Nevertheless, we were still a little concerned about the lack of guests being referred to us since we officially opened in May of that year.

On Thursday 20 October I wrote in my journal:

Norman and I prayed about this on Tuesday evening. I asked God if I had got it all wrong. Was He waiting on something? Did I need to do something? Why were people not coming?

Well, as I read Habakkuk 2:2-3 this morning, I believe I got my answer:

'Write the vision and make it plain on tablets, that he may run who reads it. For the vision is yet for an appointed time, but at the end it will speak and it will not lie. Though it tarries, wait for it, because it will surely come. It will not tarry.'

Then I read the Kingdom Dynamics at the bottom of the page in my Bible:

'Hearing the voice of God is the birth right of the believer.' Like Habakkuk, we can take a posture before God that enables us to hear his voice.

Meet with the Lord regularly in a special place of prayer. 'I will stand my watch.'

Look for God to speak to us in visions and dreams. I will 'watch to see.'

Listen for the word of the Lord. 'He will say to me.'

Keep a journal of things that God says. 'Write the vision.'

Wait for God to bring it to pass. 'It will surely come.'

Then I went on to read Habakkuk 3:17-19 including the 'word wealth' on the word 'JOY' and it is just for me. Verse 19 says 'The LORD is my strength. He will make my feet like deer's feet, and He will make me walk on my high hills.'

So I really believe God has spoken to me today and answered my petition. I will rejoice and be glad and know that my God will bring it all to pass at the right time.

The following Wednesday I wrote:

I do feel quite alone sometimes. Today was one of those days. I was allowing the enemy to get at me. I was reading 2 Timothy 4 today and it really encouraged me. The moment I definitely commit myself, then God moves also, and a whole stream of events begin. All manner of unforeseen incidents, meetings, people and material assistance which I never dreamed of begin to move towards me. When others refuse to go with you, commitment means going on alone. Daniel dined and prayed alone. Elijah sacrificed and witnessed alone. Jeremiah prophesied and wept alone. It's at the point of commitment, and not before, that God intervenes on our behalf. Continue to be strong. Be tirelessly faithful in those things God has commissioned you to do. Those words really spoke to me.

In my *Streams in the Desert* book which I read every day, it says exactly the same. Jesus wanted to be alone with his Father so that He could face the day and the challenges ahead of Him. So how much more do I need to spend time alone with my Father. When we feel alone, we need to come to our Father and be built up ready to carry on the good work He has ordained for us to do. If we don't do it, who will? You see. I told you He always encourages me. I feel encouraged already as I spend my time with Him. He confirms and encourages me to keep going. All is well.

And these were my reflections on Thursday 27 October:

In my daily reading today from UCB I read 'Your breakthrough.' It was Micah 2:3 and so apt for me: 'The One who breaks open the way will go up before you.'

God is so encouraging. The reading is just for me. It goes on to say 'When everything around you starts to shake and your fear level skyrockets, you're not about to crash and burn, you're on the threshold of a breakthrough.'

How good is that? I take that for myself today.

On 31 October the electrician, the plumber and the heating company all came on the same day. A bit like buses – you wait ages for one to come, then all three come at once! We crossed a few things off our to-do list – new light fittings in the bottom corridor, everything PAT tested and the leak in the bathroom basin fixed. And we added one for Warners to sort out – the thermostat for the heating didn't work so it was either on full or it was off. I got excited when Mark (our electrician) came and put some electric sockets in the Lilac room. The bedside light made it so much more homely and it suddenly seemed as if there was life in that room; not just light but life.

* * *

During 2011 we had two significant celebrations – our Ruby Wedding Anniversary (forty years!) and my sixtieth birthday! We spent our anniversary with all the family and had a meal out together at a restaurant in Spalding. To celebrate my birthday, I invited my family and friends to The Well Head Centre for 'Afternoon Tea'. I didn't want any gifts, but people could give a donation to The Centre if they wished. Around sixty guests shared the day with me. Mr Tickle played the piano for us and I showed people around and they were all very excited to see how far we had come.

Two days later on my actual birthday (13th December) I went for some much-needed prayer from the team in the Healing Rooms. I needed to get some direction and guidance from the Lord as I was feeling a little discouraged and wondering if I had got it all wrong and that was the reason people weren't coming into The Well Head Centre. I just wanted some answers to keep me steadfast in this project. As well as words of wisdom and encouragement I received three pictures from our faithful intercessors:

The first was of Jesus standing just around the corner saying, 'Follow Me, I will guide you.' In the second I was sitting down under an acacia tree just resting in the Lord. The third was a stream with trees all along the sides and God saying, 'I will refresh you.'

These pictures really spoke to me. I felt able to look forward to 2012 and all that God had in store for us.

Health, wealth and another leak!

As they drank their wine at the banquet, the king said to Esther, 'What is your petition, for it shall be granted to you. And what is your request? Even to half of the kingdom it shall be done.' Esther 5:6

'No! I don't believe it!' I said as I stared into my cup, having drained the last mouthful of coffee. 'There's a pound coin in here!' Margaret (one of our team) and I were having a lunch break during the National Association of Healing Rooms Conference in Halifax in April 2012. Later in the break another member of our team joined us. 'Drink anyone?' she asked. 'I'll have another coffee please,' I said. 'Here, take this,' and I handed her the pound coin I'd just fished out of my coffee cup. 'Well, Margaret. I wanted to sow that pound coin as a seed in the offering tonight as you suggested but now I've gone and spent it on two cups of coffee!' As I said this, two men around our table who had been listening to the conversation both simultaneously took a one-pound coin out of their pockets and put them on the table in front of us. So I now had two coins to put in the offering bucket during the evening meeting. My money had already doubled! But it didn't end there. As the bucket was coming round we suddenly noticed another pound coin on Norman's lap, so we added that to our offering as well.

At that same conference we gave a short presentation on The Well Head Centre to about 200 delegates. A gentleman who was sitting on the row just in front of us said to me afterwards that I was like Esther (in the Bible). So, when I got home, I reread the book of Esther and it reminded me of all the favour she received from the King. I reflected on this in my journal:

> Many times when we were preparing to set up The Well Head Centre, people said that I was like Esther and would receive favour. I know this to be true. God

has been so good to us. I always ask God to tell me something three times if it is from Him so I don't miss anything He has to say to me and I now know that His favour is on me.

On a church retreat a month later, one of my closest friends said that she had a picture she wanted to share with me. It was of a chest with gold coins in it and they were being tipped out into a well.

On our way home from the retreat Norman told me that he had been speaking to the man who is part of the organisation in Peterborough who was key in us receiving the £5,000 for The Well Head Centre last year. He told Norman that if we applied again we could receive a similar amount for this year too.

I wrote in my journal:

I truly believe God is confirming that He is Jehovah Jireh, our Provider, and that we shall prosper in all we do for Him. I also believe that it means people. People coming into The Well Head Centre. Broken lives healed. Also, treasure means wisdom and knowledge of heaven, so I am believing for all this too.

During that year we certainly did experience God's blessings. We added more referrers to our list – some Stamford Macmillan Nurses, a couple of ladies from the United Reformed Church, a lady from The Evergreen Care Trust and the pastor from New Life Church, Sleaford – and by the end of the year we had forty-nine referrers. Those who came to see the Centre were amazed and excited by what we were doing which encouraged us greatly.

Slowly but surely this led to guests starting to book in – many arrived broken, worn down and in need of recovery but left refreshed, healed and restored.

We were often amazed and humbled by people's willingness to give generously both financially and in prayer support. And we were touched by the smaller but no less special acts of kindness such as one guest giving us a new CD player and a box of bathroom goodies and a referrer giving us a box of biscuits to share with the guests. All through the year, donations steadily came in and in July some of the 100+ Prayer Army Team from our church (KingsGate) came to see what they were praying for each month and were amazed at God's provision for the place. And, though it might seem hard to believe, we even had some encouragement from the HMRC:

28th February: We can now claim Gift Aid as from October 4th 2011. We are really pleased about that. It means we can claim 25p for every £1 given so that will be a great help to our financial position. Praise God.

From all this, it seemed only right that we should bless others as we had been blessed. At the Trustees Meeting in April we decided to give three worthy organisations £500 each from our tithe:

A children's home in Zimbabwe
An orphanage in India
Thorpe Hall, a Hospice in Peterborough.

I wrote in my journal:

We know the money will be spent wisely. We also know that as we bless others, we too are blessed. God is so good. I love to send out cheques to worthy causes.

Monday 16 January saw the arrival of our first guest that year. She really enjoyed her first day and told us later that she felt a great weight had been lifted off her and that The Well Head Centre was a peaceful place. On Thursday she and one of the volunteers both enjoyed a back massage. When she left on the Saturday she looked totally different and told us that she had had an amazing time during her stay with us. On her 'Guest Feedback' form she said it had been a life-saver for her and that she would tell everyone about The Centre. We were amazed, shocked and stunned.

With each new guest we learnt new things. One guest in February only stayed twenty-four hours as that is all the time she had available. Nevertheless, she had a wonderful time and really benefitted from her stay. We had always thought one day wouldn't be long enough so we learnt a valuable lesson that God can work in people's lives even in a short space of time. When a couple of guests left after their stay in October they said that they felt like they had been 'cocooned' whilst with us.

Nevertheless, we encountered our fair share of niggles and setbacks in 2012 as well. On Sunday 12th February while enjoying a lovely lunch in a village pub I noticed a voicemail message on my mobile phone. It was Anglian Water telling me that there had been a leak in our boiler room and water was coming under the boiler room doors and running down the street! I thought 'Oh no, not again.' We hurried back and surveyed the damage. The very low temperatures we had experienced a few nights' ago had frozen the capped pipe and then the rapid thaw that morning had blasted the cap off. There was water halfway up one wall and all over the floor too. I was concerned about the central heating boiler. If that had tried to come on in the night with no water circulating then that could have done a lot of damage. We needed a quick solution! Mark from Warners came to the rescue and within ten minutes one of his fitters came and put the cap back on for us. When he turned the water back on everything was OK.

Panic over! Thank the Lord for the person who was walking past and noticed something was wrong this morning and actually did something about it. And that we will not have to pay for all the wasted water as we don't yet have a water meter! Our God is an awesome God. He is always watching over us.

In April we received two bills from the district council for non-domestic rates for 2011 and 2012. One was for £2,000 and one for £5,000. I was shocked and dumbfounded. I was angry and confused. I just had to walk away and leave Norman the job of contacting them about this. He understands the council better than me, having worked in a local authority for so many years! It turned out that we hadn't been allowed the 80% mandatory relief for being a registered charity. Anyway, a few hours later, when I had calmed down, Norman told me the council were going to send us two more bills as they had made a mistake. That was a relief!

Apart from the leak and confusion over bills there were further legal and practical hoops to climb through. In January we had the Health and Safety Officer from South Kesteven District Council to check everything over and she listed a few things we needed to put in place by April to cover ourselves and our guests staying overnight in the bungalow. Also one of our trustees came around to do a 'Risk Assessment' for Fire, Health and Safety but thankfully there were only a few minor adjustments we needed to make to come up to scratch. In March we had an 'Asbestos Survey' of the bungalow which went well with no issues.

In October and again in November the plumber came to make good all the pipes in the Healing Rooms end of the bungalow that were capped off three years ago when we took out all the basins and the redundant toilet. We were told that there could be a risk of salmonella or legionnaires disease if we didn't have ten pipes capped off in the loft too. After his visit he sent us a letter as the official paperwork to show we had had the proper work done so there is no health risk for any of our guests.

My own health, however, suffered that year. In January I had high blood pressure. The ECG and blood tests came back as normal but the doctor put me on a low dose and then increased it to a higher dose for several months. At the same time I had a horrible virus – my chest was rattling and hurting quite a bit and I had never coughed so much in my life!

By early March I was feeling more myself. I had finally got my energy back and I wasn't coughing as much. I felt encouraged when I read a message in my UCB Daily Reading entitled 'Refuse to Pull Back':

It was just what I needed to hear today. I believe the Lord gave me a shot in the arm to buck me up and get me back on track again. It was basically saying that Satan will try any scheme or thought to put fear into us about things that are not even likely to happen. His goal is to try and stop us dead in our tracks. He knows God's plan is for us to 'spread out to the right and to the left' and not to pull back. What I need to do is remember to always put on the full armour of God, so that I may be able to stand in the evil day, and to stand on God's Word. His word says this....

'Enlarge the place of your tent, stretch your tent curtains wide, do not hold back. Lengthen your cords, strengthen your stakes. For you will spread out to the right hand and to the left. Do not be afraid, you will not suffer shame. Do not fear disgrace. You will not be humiliated.'

I take this on board today and will keep meditating on it until I get full revelation of His word and His promises to me. This all comes from Isaiah chapter 54.

Amanda has just sent me this text too from Philippians 4:13. 'For I can do everything through Christ, who gives me strength.'

The other health problem came about when we were at the Edinburgh Military Tattoo in Scotland in August. At the end of a lovely evening I hurt my foot when stepping off the bottom step of the tiered seating as it was unexpectedly deeper than the rest. I was in quite a lot of pain. The GP thought it could be a torn ligament and if that were the case then it could take even longer to heal than a broken bone. She told me to rest it as much as possible and to put some inflammatory gel on it.

One prayer time I thought I heard God say to me 'fallen arches'! When I had a hairline fracture in my ankle a little while ago the specialist said that I needed to be careful as my arches were falling down.

When I went to see the physiotherapist on 2nd October she confirmed both the torn ligament and the fallen arches. By this point my foot had been painful for about six weeks. I had tried everything, listened to everyone, had prayer for it, a prayer cloth sent and still it didn't seem to be getting any better. The physio gave me an A4 sheet of paper with light exercises to do and told me to put a cold compress on for ten minutes then a hot one for ten minutes and to get some insoles for my shoes to help with the fallen arches.

I am now praying and believing for total healing of my foot.

But healing seemed slow in coming:

> Wednesday 10 October: I went to do my shopping today in the town. As I was walking I was in so much pain. Every time I put my right foot down I was in pain. I was hobbling around like an old woman. It was all too much for me. I went into our local cobblers just to see if I could get a pair of shoes with some good support and with spongy heels and soles to help me when walking on hard surfaces. I cried most of the time doing my shopping. I had taken one of my tablets which is supposed to take away any inflammation, but it wasn't working today.

On 23 October I received more prayer for my foot and went to see my physiotherapist again. She told me 'We need to get it moving as it has seized up and is now swollen. You must use it or lose it.' That was like a bolt of lightning to me. I was determined not to lose it, so I made sure I did everything she had suggested after that.

On Saturday 3 November I wrote:

> My foot seems to be a lot better today. We have been away in the Cotswolds for three days and it seems to have done it some good. I can put a little more weight on it so I believe we are on the mend. Hallelujah! Praise God for my healing.

This was good news as I could enjoy riding my new bike – a 'Special Edition Jubilee' in red, white and blue with mud guards called

'Duchess'. We had each bought one from the garden centre a few weeks before as early Christmas presents to each other and were enjoying our new hobby.

God continued to encourage us that year through prayers, pictures, words, quiet times and ministry. On 19th January, after Healing Rooms had finished, two ladies wanted to pray for me. One of them said they saw a picture of a white dove dragging a large net behind it. She felt it was God saying that many people are coming into The Well Head Centre. That was very encouraging to me. The other lady said that God was going to open a new door for me. One that I could never dream of. So that will be exciting too.

In June at our first Healing Rooms Regional Training Day in Nottingham we gave a short talk about The Well Head Centre and handed out about fifty of our flyers. While we were there a lady had a word for me. She took me aside and said that she saw me as Florence Nightingale, a nurse who went to places no-one else wanted to go and helped those who were left all alone. She did pioneering work.

I wrote in my journal:

> I believe this is true of me and God is helping me to accomplish this.

On 6th December I was getting a little discouraged by not many guests coming to the Centre so in my prayer time with the Lord, I asked Him if He would encourage me. When I got to my computer I came across an email from a lady who had stayed with us earlier in the year. She said that as she was praying for us she had a picture, and in this picture she saw a desert and people were travelling from afar on their camels to be replenished. She said she got the sense that people are en route, but they have a long way to go first.

I recorded in my journal:

> I am really encouraged by this and know that they will come and in fact are on their way. Praise God. He is so good to me.

Further encouragement came from a friend at church that Sunday who wanted to pray for me:

She told me not to be downcast or discouraged, as the guests will come. She also told me that it appears that when I pray there seems to be a wall there. Well she has just seen Jesus take me by the hand and walk me around that wall as if it wasn't even there. I hadn't told her anything about how I was feeling!! God always puts the right people across my path.

On Saturday 15 December in my daily readings in *Streams in the Desert* I read:

'In spite of our feelings and evidence to the contrary, and even when we cannot understand our way or our situation, may we still "Trust also in Him, for He shall bring it to pass." The way will open, our situation will be changed, and the end result will be peace. The cloud will finally be lifted and the light of eternal noonday will shine at last.'

'Trust and rest when all around you
Puts your faith to the test.
Let no fear or foe confound you,
Wait for God and trust and rest.
Trust and rest with heart abiding,
Like a birdling in its nest.
Underneath its feathers hiding.
Fold your wings and trust and rest.'

I really needed to hear that not just because of the disappointments over the small numbers coming to the Centre but because we had recently had the sad news of one of our faithful volunteers passing away. Natalie had been suffering with cancer for about two years. We miss her greatly. She brought so much when she was with us. We planted a rose bush in the garden at the front of The Well Head Centre when we first heard about her illness and were told that she didn't have long to live. The Lord gave her another year and so she had time to see her rose in flower. It is called 'Pure Gold' and that is what Natalie was. We can remember Natalie every year now and it will always bring back lovely memories of her time with us.

Two particular family events stand out from 2012. In June a man from the Salvation Army in Bourne gave me a package and told me it contained information about my Great Grandad, Isaac, on my mum's side. I found out that my Grandad's Father committed suicide at the age of thirty-nine by taking rat poison and his wife ended up in a mental asylum. This was my response:

I was saddened yet touched as I believe it has been placed in my heart to help such as these. It is in my DNA, so to speak. That is why The Well Head Centre is so close to my heart. It has confirmed so much to me about this project. God wants to use me to help those who are on the edge. He wants me to help bring them back. He will be glorified in The Well Head Centre. People's lives will be changed for His Glory.

In late August we stayed the weekend at our daughter Hazel's. We were thrilled when she told us that two of her boys – Zach aged seven and Ben aged five – gave their hearts to the Lord on their way to church the previous Sunday. Hazel said the conversation went a bit like this.

Zach: 'Mummy, how do people hear from God?'

Mummy: 'Well when you become a Christian, Jesus comes to live in your heart and so you can hear Him better because He is inside you.'

Zach: 'Could I become a Christian?'

Mummy: 'Yes Zach. All you have to do is say a prayer and invite Jesus into your life.'

Zach: 'Well I would like to do that. Can we do it now?'

Mummy: 'Okay. Do you want to repeat after me this prayer?'

Zach: 'Yes'

Hazel's other son Ben is now interested and so says, 'Yes I do too. Make me a Christian. Make me a Christian!'

Zach: 'Shall we close our eyes while we pray?'

Mummy: 'Well you can, but I won't as I am driving!'

Hazel said the prayer while also concentrating on driving and Zach and Ben repeated it after her.

Then Zach said, 'What about the Holy Spirit?'

Mummy: 'Do you want to receive the Holy Spirit too?'

Zach: 'Ooooh yes!'

So Hazel prayed for them to receive the Holy Spirit and Zach said, 'Oooooh Mummy, I feel all tingly and I can't stop smiling.'

The boys couldn't wait to tell us about this as soon as we arrived last Friday afternoon.

Zach also said that he had had his first answer to prayer. He had been having bad dreams, so he prayed to God and asked for some nice dreams instead. Hazel had also been praying for him to have funny dreams that would make him giggle. Well Zach had a funny dream and when he tried to tell his mum about it he just couldn't stop giggling. It was so funny.

During the weekend while we were staying there Hazel developed a headache, I hurt my ankle and Matt (our son-in-law) had a painful back and so both Zach and Ben prayed for us all. They did it with so much love and compassion. They are mighty boys for God and will grow up to be mighty men of God.

* * *

Following on from our time away we took part in several events. On August 29th we had a very successful day making contacts at the One Event (formerly Grapevine) on the showground in Lincoln. We gave out loads of our flyers and were invited to give a talk on the showground radio whilst there. Talk about getting thrown in at the deep end!

In September Norman and I had a stand at two further networking events. The first was the 'First Contact Fayre' in Stamford. We put up our 'pop up' banner with all our details on and a three-section display board with photos of the rooms and gardens at The Well Head Centre, plus some feedback from some of our guests.

At first we had a room upstairs but all the action seemed to be happening downstairs so we asked if we could set up on one of the empty tables there instead. It was buzzing downstairs – lots of people and a good atmosphere. We made lots of contacts. We had seven people who wanted to be referrers and signed up to receive all our details.

The second event was the Network Peterborough Christian Conference. David and Gill helped us all day. We made a lot of contacts, some of whom came to our 'Open House' event in October. One vicar from a church in Peterborough wanted to donate some money to us, which was a real blessing.

A different kind of publicity happened that autumn in the form of a radio broadcast:

8th October: I received a call from the lady at Radio Cambridgeshire today. She is coming over on Saturday to our 'Open House' event and wants to have a chat with me about doing a live telephone conversation on the Sunday morning programme at 8.00am. WOW, WOW, WOW! I am looking forward to it, I think, but a bit nervous too.

Sunday 28 October: Well I did my chat over the radio this morning. It seemed to go really well, I thought! David and Gill who tuned in to hear it gave us a call to say it was great. I pray that God will use that chat to make people realise how important it is to take time out when things are getting too much for them to cope with and that there is a place where they can go.

To close this chapter I want to return to the scripture we opened with. Many times during 2012 I felt like Esther must have done when the king asked her what she wanted and generously offered her up to half his kingdom. The king granted Esther's request and God responded to ours:

Thursday 22 November: I was given £102 today as a gift to The Well Head Centre. You know, God is so faithful. I am amazed more and more at His kindness towards us. He is surely Jehovah Jireh, our Provider. It is proven in all He has done for us and is providing for us, and it keeps coming. Everywhere people want to give me money or things that are needed. I was given a box of snowdrop bulbs from my next-door neighbour last week for us to plant in the gardens. God thinks about everything. Every little detail He provides for. When I need something I remember Esther 5:6 and I claim it and then go and ask. God is so amazing. I love to watch Him work things out for us. He does it much better than I could! I trust Him completely in every area of my life.

Feet like a deer

'Fig trees may no longer bloom, or vineyards produce grapes, olive trees may be fruitless, and harvest time a failure, sheep pens may be empty, and cattle stalls vacant but I will still celebrate because the LORD God is my Saviour. The LORD gives me strength. He makes my feet as sure as those of a deer, and He helps me stand on the mountains.' Habakkuk 3:17-19 CEV.

On 6th January I wrote in my journal:

I believe in 2013 things will change. The floodgates will open. We shall have an explosion of guests wanting to come and stay with us. I believe it. I declare it. I call it into being. I call those things that are not as though they were.

God seemed to confirm this in February when a friend from church said that she saw a tsunami coming over me! Yet as the days and weeks passed by with very few bookings I got discouraged. One day in early March I spent the morning praying and worshipping God.

That evening Norman told me what one of our intercessors had said to him at Healing Rooms after he had told her that I was getting a little anxious about things:

'I have a plaque on my wall at home and it says this "things of worth take time to grow." There will be a time when The Well Head Centre will be full.' So I took this as an answer from God and continued to wait and trust Him.

On Tuesday 2 April I wrote:

I am still waiting for the floodgates to open, the phone to ring and the emails to come flooding in!

Although this didn't happen immediately a number of other things encouraged us at that time. On 4th January I had a phone call from a lady who came to stay with us last June for one night. She wanted to let us know how much her stay with us had helped her. 'I've just had the most amazing Christmas,' she told me. 'Normally I hate Christmas and New Year. Often I've wanted to end my life. But this year I feel so different. I'm so happy I could explode. I'm going around telling everyone how I feel because I've never felt this way before!'

Also on 18th January we had a meeting with Philip Warner. Our lease was due to run out in September that year but after some discussion he said that he was willing to extend the lease for another three years. Praise God!

In February Alison and I went to a four-day Healing Conference in Cardiff. We had a wonderful time – people prayed for us, prophesied over us and encouraged us all the time. We received an anointing and impartation from the Healing Rooms team from Bethel Church in Redding, California and Tom Jones (not 'THE' Tom Jones) was one of the main speakers! I was so blessed by their ministry. We felt refreshed and built up in the Lord – a precious time we shall never forget.

* * *

Although we didn't have people coming in droves, we started to see the transformation that was happening in those who did come to stay with us.

Saturday 16 February: We had a lovely time with our guest over the last two days. She painted three pictures whilst she was with us and she serenaded us on her guitar too! We really loved her stay with us and I believe it did her the world of good too. It always amazes me how very different all our guests are but how they all need some time out. Time to re-group, time to rest, time to relax, time to just be themselves and time to re-discover life again. How it was originally intended to be. Not cluttered and

busy but quiet, restful and meaningful. I'm so glad
we can provide a place for this to happen.

With any new venture you are on a steep learning curve and we continued to have incidents and setbacks along the way. One of these occurred in early February when we had guests staying. I went into the laundry room to put a loaf of bread in the freezer and noticed a funny smell. I happened to touch one of the bread loaves and it felt squidgy. I felt another and it was the same! I checked the temperature gauge and it was showing ten degrees. It should read minus twenty degrees ! I phoned the insurance company in a panic. The man said they would send someone on Monday. I immediately said, 'I'm sorry, I need someone here today. We are a charity and we have people staying here.' In the end he agreed someone would be around between twelve and six o'clock. I thanked him profusely. In the meantime, Carol (one of our volunteers) and I had to start emptying the freezer which was full of bread, pies, soup, ice-cream and other stuff. I was going to throw most of it away until one of our guests said she could take the bread for her chickens who would love it! So I put loads of bread in a black plastic sack and gave it to her. We then had to dry everywhere up. There were bucket loads to mop up including the floor.

Later that morning while having a well-deserved coffee and rest, I suddenly had a thought: had the freezer been switched off by mistake? I don't know where that thought came from, but I did know that the previous week we had had all our appliances PAT tested by our friendly electrician. I went to check. The socket was switched off! I felt so embarrassed. I immediately switched it back on and it started humming again. Anyway, when the engineer came at six o'clock, I apologised profusely and told him what had happened. He didn't seem to mind as it meant he could go home early.

The one lonely loaf of bread left after that episode was a lesson learnt: remember to check the sockets each time we have our appliances tested from now on.

On another occasion the microwave decided to play up. It kept on cooking even though the pinger had gone off. We had a guest staying so we needed to replace it quickly. Some months previously we'd had a conversation with a man who worked in one of the undertakers here in Bourne. 'If you need help in any way, just give me a ring,' he'd said. We decided to take him at his word and within a few hours we had a brand-new microwave! Once more God had provided for our needs.

Although things were a bit quiet in terms of guests, we were kept busy with publicity events and pursued every avenue we could to get the message out there about The Centre and to add more referrers to our ever-growing list.

In January three events stand out: the interview we did in October of the previous year was broadcast by Cambridgeshire Radio, two ladies came from the Rape Crisis Team in Peterborough and promised to see if any of their clients met our criteria and Norman and I had a stand at the Ground Level Leaders Meeting in Lincoln New Life Church. We made some new contacts on the day of the event and this generated a stream of emails in the following days, which was very encouraging. By 14th January we had fifty-nine referrers.

In February Norman and I went to speak to the Adult Social Care Team at the County Offices in Sleaford, Lincolnshire. There were eleven ladies there and they just loved what they heard about our Centre. At the end of our talk all eleven of them wanted to be added to our list of referrers. I wrote in my journal:

> We now have seventy-seven referrers. God is definitely on the move. That is the most we have ever added to our list in one day.

We also went to a meeting of pastors and leaders at our church in Peterborough. We gave a short presentation which seemed to be well received and left them with a load of flyers to pass on to their Life Group Leaders. A few days later Norman told me that all the Group Pastors were now going to be referrers to The Well Head Centre. An encouraging result!

On Friday 19 April we had our first 'Open House' event for potential referrers. Thirteen people attended and they were all blown away by what they saw. Some were even moved to tears when looking around and hearing some of the stories of how it all came into being.

During April Norman went to a 'Carers Convention' and in May we had a stand at a 'First Contact' meeting in Surfleet, Lincolnshire. By 15th May I noted in my journal:

> We now have fifteen partners each giving financially to The Well Head Centre each month. God is so good. We now also have one hundred and eight names on our referrer's list. That sounds good, but we now need them to start referring!

It had been a very cold winter so we had almost given up hope of it ever being warm enough to work on the water feature in the quad area of the garden that Katherine had designed for us all those years ago. But in April, on the warmest day we'd had so far that year, Margaret and Brian came armed with their tools, muscle power and good humour and completed it in just one day. We now have a beautiful mound approximately three feet high by four feet wide with small plants dotted around. There is a concrete sort of slide from top to bottom so the water cascades down onto some large pebbles and down into a large container where the electric pump circulates it back up to the top. It just goes round and round and makes a lovely refreshing, peaceful and relaxing sound for guests when in the garden. I am so looking forward to switching it on for them.

* * *

At times we saw God intervene in the tiniest details of our lives at the exact moment we needed something. In June we had a wonderful week at The Centre. We had a pastor and his wife for a couple of days; a lady from Peterborough from Monday through to Sunday; a lady from Monday to Friday and another from Thursday to Sunday. They all really enjoyed their stay with us. The weather was glorious. We enjoyed a flower arranging session with one of our volunteers and one of our guests had a painting session with other guests. However, a funny thing happened when one of our guests arrived on the Thursday. I took her to her room and left her there to get her things sorted. When she wanted to come out and lock her door she got the lock stuck somehow! She couldn't unlock it again. All of her stuff was locked inside her room and she was standing outside her door panicking. Her partner tried and he couldn't do it. They called me to have a go and I couldn't do it either. I decided to phone Warners to see if anyone could come over and sort this problem out for us. They said they could but it would probably ruin the lock. I had a long hard think about the situation. I said, 'Let's pray about this.' So we did and then we had another go at the lock. It freed up and we could open the door. I immediately called Warners to say that it had been sorted. We were all so happy and totally amazed.

A similar incident had happened the previous September. One of our newest guests, a young lady with long, flowing hair approached me in the corridor. 'Oh, Janice,' she said. 'I wonder if you have a rubber band about the place. I'd like to put my hair up while I'm in the shower and I forgot to bring anything suitable.' Our storeroom has all sorts in it but I knew I hadn't seen a rubber band in there or anywhere else in the bungalow for that matter.

'Hmm . . . I'm sorry. I don't think I have any rubber bands.'

'Never mind,' she said. 'I will just use straighteners when I come out.'

After a while, Norman and I went outside to get something from the car. When we got back to the front door there was a rubber band on the floor.

'Look, Norman! God has dropped a rubber band from heaven for us. We can go and give it to our guest now.'

Norman calmly replied 'It didn't drop from heaven, Jan. The postman dropped it after he had delivered our post.'

I was a little deflated but then I realised that God will use anyone to fulfil His purposes and He wanted us to lack nothing. I immediately took it to our guest and explained what had happened. She was totally shocked and amazed. God's timing is always perfect.

* * *

We returned to the verses in Habakkuk frequently that year reminding ourselves that the Lord was our strength. Hebrews 10:35-36 also spoke to me:

'Therefore, do not cast away your confidence which has great reward. For you have need of endurance, so that after you have done the will of God, you may receive the promise.'

And God also spoke to us through several pictures others had for us:

Sunday 19 May: A friend at church told me that she had a picture whilst praying for me today. It was of a watering can! She said that God was telling me to keep watering the seeds I have sown and to keep on watering ...

... Tuesday 9 July: At the Healing Rooms today someone had a picture for me. In the picture I was walking and a great wind was howling around me. Large boulders were being thrown but Jesus had His arms around me. He is protecting me and says to me 'keep going forward for I am with you, I am holding you up.' It really encouraged me to keep going. Bless God ...

Verse 19 of Habakkuk 3 where it talks about making our feet like those of a deer were also significant as I continued to have problems with my feet. A scan in March revealed I had a strained ligament so I had to have some physiotherapy at the Bourne Health Centre. Here are some entries from my journal about this:

Friday 5 April: Today I have been reading all the scriptures I can find relating to the 'feet' and 'smooth paths' as I am still in a little discomfort with my right ankle. I have had loads of prayer and I have now just been for my first session of physiotherapy. The next appointment is in six weeks. I told the guy that

I am reading all the scriptures I can relating to the feet and I think that is making the difference. He looked at me a bit funny and then said 'OK, I'll see you again in six weeks.' I have come off the Naproxin (painkillers and anti-inflammatory tablets) I was taking because I know it is getting much better. I also read Habakkuk 3:17-19 again as it especially applies to The Well Head centre right now...

...Tuesday 14 May: Last week I went to see the physiotherapist again. He asked me how I had got on and if things were any better. I told him again that I was a Christian and that I had been reading verses from the Bible about the FEET and that I believed that my foot was now healed. I hadn't been doing the exercises much so I am sure that that wasn't the reason my foot was now healed! Then he said to me 'Would you like some more exercises to do?' So I replied 'No thanks. I'll be fine.' So he then said 'Okay. I'll give you a call in six to twelve weeks just to see how you are getting on.' So that was that! I keep reading and declaring healing over my foot every day. I believe the word of God is the best medicine. I'm healed by Jesus stripes. Praise God...

...Sunday 19 May: I do now believe that my right foot is totally healed. We went for a really long walk in Bourne woods last Thursday. I did enjoy it. My foot did ache a bit in the evening but nothing like the pain I had been experiencing. It is so good to get out of bed in the morning and be able to put pressure on both my feet equally and to walk down the stairs normally again. God is so good.

By the summer more and more guests started to come and the diary started to fill up with bookings. On Sunday 28 July I wrote in my journal:

We had a female guest in all last week. We are now getting ready for the three guests we have booked in tomorrow for the week. We have also got two ladies booked in for August, so I think things are picking up.

One of those guests was a lovely 54-year-old lady who was self-harming. Whilst she was staying with us she went out for a walk in the park which is just next door. This one particular day as she was walking, she noticed some broken glass glistening on the floor. She stopped and looked at it with the intention of picking it up and using it to harm herself. She was planning on bringing it back to The Centre and using it to harm herself during the night. This is what the voices were telling her to do as she was a bad girl. Well just as she was about to bend down and pick up the broken glass, she heard God's voice say to her 'Don't pick that up and let yourself down and all those at The Well Head Centre.' So she just walked off and left it there on the ground. She told me this the next day. I was so relieved and proud of her for doing that and for telling us about it too. As I wrote in my diary at the time:

I believe that is the first step to her recovery. She has many scars and open wounds on both her arms. I prayed for her and declared total healing in the name of Jesus. I believe she is now well on her way to a full recovery. Praise God.

With more guests we had plenty of ongoing jobs to do: lawns to mow, carpets to clean and floors to mop; sheets to wash and iron plus admin tasks and responding to emails.

In the midst of all this we had a visit from a lady from the Lincolnshire Fire Service. She found quite a few things that weren't to her liking! So added to our list were the following things which we needed to achieve in the next three months:

Put a lock on the storeroom door.

Add a door closure on the laundry room door plus a fire strip all around it.

Make sure all the bedroom doors close by themselves.

Take down the curtain at the front door as it is a fire hazard and replace it with either a roller blind or some dark film.

I felt a bit deflated after all that.

But thanks to our trusted workmen we had everything done by the end of September: Peter K put a door closure on the laundry room door and a lock on the COSHH cupboard (Control of Substances Hazardous to Health). Mark, our electrician friend and his mate added another sounder to the bungalow and checked the decibel levels in all the bedrooms. Peter (our carpenter) came to check that all the bedroom doors closed properly on their own.

We had more publicity in the summer months when an article about The Well Head Centre was published in the 'Lincolnshire Carers Partnerships' monthly newsletter, then another in 'Carers Connect' and a third in 'Rethink' in their quarterly magazine. The number of referrers continued to grow and we added several more people to our 'Prayer Support Team' who prayed faithfully for everything that went on each month at the Healing Rooms and The Well Head Centre. We also continued to receive donations, something that had happened every month since we opened in July 2011. What a faithful God we have!

In September a young lady came to stay with us. Before she came, she was ready to walk out on her husband and children:

She loved art and painting and so made a few visits to 'Paint a Pot' in the town. She found this to be relaxing, rewarding and inspiring.

She had intended to stay until Sunday morning but on Friday she told us that she was ready to go back to face things again and that she was missing her children. She wanted to see her children the following evening just before they went to bed and then spend the evening with her husband. And she wanted to spend Sunday with all the family together before the working week on Monday.

When she left, she gave us an 8-inch 'Thank you' tile which she had painted at 'Paint a Pot'. She wrote on the tile as if it was a card. It was lovely. She also told us that we saved her marriage. We know it was God who had saved her marriage. We are so pleased for her. It is great when our guests want to go home early because the work has been done.

In October we had a two-week holiday in Canada. The first week we spent in Toronto and attended a 'Catch the Fire' conference. We both had prophetic words spoken over us. Norman was told 'It is Christmas, so expect gifts.' In other words, favour and blessing. We feel we already have it! I was told that God wanted to pour out His gifts, blessings and favour on us both. He wanted to give me diamonds. So I am looking for them to fall on me! We met some lovely people and we were both re-ignited.

We also visited Niagara Falls again. This time we had a trip on 'The Maid of the Mist', which goes right up to the falls. It was an amazing experience – the sound of the water is truly something else! Then we went to Ottawa for a week and stayed in Norman's sister's apartment. We caught up with all his nieces and nephews and attended the wedding of his sister's youngest daughter. It was a really special time.

Shortly after our holiday we had a guest booked in who we weren't really sure fitted our criteria but we decided to take her anyway. Her referrer said she would pop in during the week just to make sure she was OK:

Well she was no trouble at all – a bit demanding at times, but no more than some others we have had! We had a great time. She was so funny. She made us laugh and we made her laugh. She got on tremendously well with Norman and was asking me where he was most of the time! She brought some jigsaws in with her and Norman helped her to do some of them. She had a motorized scooter which Norman put on charge for her every night so she could use it in the day. On her last day with us she went out and bought a large leg of lamb and a stick of Brussels. I thought she was going to cook the meal but she wanted me to do it! She wanted us to celebrate her last day with a roast dinner. We had Yorkshire puddings and roast potatoes too. It was like a banquet. It was lovely. We think she benefitted so much being with us. Norman and I learned so much from having her stay with us. It all worked out well in the end. God is so good.

* * *

Looking back over these years, I realise leaks, flooding, torrents of water (and even a tsunami!) have been a common thread. 2013 was no exception with two particular events. One was at our own house. We had been away in Canterbury for a few days and on our return, we noticed a damp patch in our kitchen ceiling. We didn't think it necessary to call anyone at that moment but just to keep our eye on it. The next morning the damp patch had grown to around two and a half feet in diameter! We were concerned as we would be in The Centre all the following week. We called the plumber and thankfully he came round that day. He found that it was a leaking pipe under the floorboards in the bathroom. He had to get to it by cutting through the kitchen ceiling. Then he drained all the central heating system off which took about three hours leaving us with a large hole in our kitchen ceiling. 'Hello Mark, I said to our electrician/plasterer. You couldn't come and do a small job for us could you ...?'

The second incident happened in the autumn, during a heavy shower of rain a great torrent of water came down into the (blocked) gutters right over the drive. David, one of our Trustees spent the next morning clearing out all the gutters of acorns, leaves, small weeds and other rubbish.

Towards the close of 2013, I sensed it was time to stop writing my journal and get on with the ministry God had called us to do. It marked the end of one phase of our journey and the beginning of another. And what a journey it had been! Highs and lows, frenetic activity and long delays, intense excitement and cruel disappointments. Yet, through it all we knew God was with us and 'we never walked alone'.

It seems appropriate to conclude with the last entry in my journal. It expresses something of the heart of our ministry:

Sunday 15 December: A guy came to stay with us a few weeks ago after visiting his GP because he was depressed. He told us that his GP didn't want to put him on anti-depressants but told him that he needed a break and some time out to think about things and where he was now heading. His GP referred him to us. He is now totally different! His stay made such an impact on him. What a transformation! This guy is the reason we opened The Well Head Centre and if it was just for this one guy, then it was all worth it.

Come full circle

May 2022

As you will be aware we have had two years of Covid-19 pandemic to contend with and the Centre has been closed for eighteen months. We reopened last September but have not had as many guests in as we hoped for. There have been many signs over the last seven months that have given us the sense that the time has come for us to close the Centre. We knew that our lease was due to end in September of this year and that Philip Warner would be letting us know if we could have it for a while longer or that he would be wanting the bungalow back. Well, we had an email from Philip letting us know that we could have it for a further twelve more months or so.

Norman and I prayed about this and sensed that it was time to close the Centre. The decision was a very hard one to make but we felt it was right.

We booked an appointment with Philip so we could have a chat about things and then we told him that we wouldn't be renewing the lease. He said, 'Well would you mind then if some of my guys come round and measure up as I have something in mind I would like to do with the bungalow?' We said, 'That is fine Philip.' Then after a short silence, he said, 'Actually Janice, since I saw the news at the weekend, I think I would like to offer the bungalow to some Ukranian Refugees. You have made this bungalow so beautiful that they could just come straight in and live in it as it is.' I was so touched. In a funny sort of way, it seemed to make it a bit easier to let it go. We have agreed to leave all the furniture, bedding and all household goods, so everything is there for them to come into and feel safe and loved. At this moment in time Ukraine is being invaded by Russia and lots of people have fled to other countries to escape the war. It seemed that God had His own plan all along and the bungalow will still be used to help hurting people. The gift just keeps on giving!

* * *

If you can remember at the very beginning of my journey, God gave me a picture of the bungalow near to where we lived and Alison and I prayed round it and claimed it. Amanda, Alison and I then went to see Mr Warner to have a chat with him about us possibly using the bungalow for a Healing Centre. When we came out of our meeting, I said, 'I believe we have planted a seed here today and it is going to grow into a beautiful tree and bear much fruit for His Kingdom.' We all agreed. Then Alison went to a prayer meeting at her church in the evening and at the end of the meeting someone stood up and said, 'I don't know who this is for, but someone has planted an acorn today and it is going to grow into a beautiful oak tree and bear much fruit.' Little did we know that at the front of the bungalow was a large oak tree!

Well, the acorn has been on our logo for The Well Head Centre from day one. In fact, there have been loads of acorns dropping off the tree over the last thirteen years. Lots of them have been planted by the squirrels and we have had to dig many of them up every year otherwise we would have had even more oak trees growing in the front garden! God's timing is always perfect and you will see why now.

At the Mothers' Day Service on 27 March 2022 at the Baptist Church here in Bourne, all the ladies were given a gift to take home. This year it was a small wooden cross and yes, you've guessed it, a little wooden acorn. When Alison told me this whilst we were having coffee in one of the cafes in the town, I was so emotional. Alison is flying off to Japan very soon to be part of a mission out there. She felt called by God about five years ago, but because of Covid it has been delayed and so now she is finally going to do what God has called her to do. God brought us both together to establish the Healing Rooms and The Well Head Centre back in 2008 and now I believe He is sending us both out on other missions. I believe Alison is going to be planting her acorn in Japan and who knows what God has got planned for us here. The day Alison flew out to Japan was the day that we restarted the Healing Rooms face-to-face ministry after being closed for two years because of Covid. We feel that that too was God's perfect timing. Nothing is a coincidence with God.

I believe we have come full circle and all in God's plan and when we finally close the Charity we wait to see where and what His plans are for us. I have learnt a lot about waiting on God in the last thirteen years so I look forward with eager anticipation to all He has got planned.

I wasn't sure how to end my book when I revisited it at Christmas. I was asking God what I should write in my last chapter. Well, I think he has answered my question now, don't you?

If you were to ask me the question, if I had my life over again would I do it again, the answer would most certainly be YES. I have met so many lovely people. Some who have made an imprint on my life. I have learned so much and will never forget the experience God allowed me to do for Him.

Testimonies

Testimony 1 – Julia

I arrived at The Well Head Centre a former shell of who I really was. I was broken. I was defeated and I didn't know who I was anymore or where I was going, and I had given up all hope completely. I wasn't living, I was just existing.

Since my husband died in 2013, I sank into a deep depression. I felt my world was over and part of me had died too. For two years I struggled to face each day. I had no life left in me. I ignored how I was feeling and tried to keep things together. Things weren't easy and I kept getting devastating news. My son became ill and ended up in a coma and I got diagnosed with Hepatitis C. I thought my life was over and I couldn't take anymore. I had no support to help me through any of this. On Christmas Day 2016 I took a very large overdose. I just couldn't take life and I thought death was my only way out of all this pain and misery. I thought everyone would be better off without me. I remember after I had taken them, for the first time in years, I felt happy! Luckily, I was found and received treatment. Then I was sectioned and put on high doses of medication which made me feel numb.

Once I was released from hospital I was under the Mental Health Team and had to see a psychiatrist and therapists as well as my GP which was all very overwhelming. From the outside, people thought I was OK, but I wasn't. I was sinking further into depression. I would spend days in bed, not leaving my bedroom. I wouldn't take pride in myself, and all I kept thinking about was ways I could end it all. I didn't understand if they really knew what was wrong with me, or whether I was even on the right medication. Why wasn't I getting any better? This went on for six months. I was beginning to think that this was how my life would be forever.

One afternoon, my therapist started talking to me about The Well Head Centre and would I be interested. At that point I didn't have anything to lose! So I accepted and he got the ball rolling and a referral was made for me. When I found that I actually met the criteria for The Well Head Centre I was ready to go as I needed to escape my lonely isolated life. I was scared inside whilst packing my bags. I didn't know if I even had the courage to leave my comfort zone, but I am pleased I did.

The second I walked into The Well Head Centre, I couldn't put my finger on it, but there was something special about the place. I felt an inner calm. I felt safe, secure and most importantly, protected. The first night I fell asleep whilst reading a book and it wasn't until the next day that I realised that I hadn't taken my sleeping pill! Without it I don't normally sleep at all! On the Tuesday, I was asked if I wanted to go into The Healing Rooms for some prayer. Again, what did I have to lose! I felt a calmness, a warmth and love.

I came out of The Healing Rooms and I remember talking to Janice and telling her that I wanted to let God back into my life. I wanted to open my heart to allow Him in. It was a very emotional time for me and one I will never forget. At the moment I gave my life to the Lord, my life changed forever. I started coming out of my room so much more whilst I was at The Well Head Centre and talking to Janice and Norman. They helped me to build up my trust and to face things that had been hidden away for many years. For once, I didn't dread waking up each day.

I started going for short walks around the area close to The Centre. I felt free, free from my mind. Whereas before I couldn't escape from the dark place I was in. My demons and the cruel things that haunted me. I would keep telling myself over and over again.

There is nowhere like The Well Head Centre. The help and non-judgemental support you receive there is unique. If you go to any hospital or clinic you have to see a team of people who are quick to diagnose you and tell you what is wrong with you. Then you get given a label put on you. Rather than recovering you start thinking you are crazy or you are so ill you won't get better. You have to accept what they say. It doesn't give you reassurance. What you receive at The Well Head Centre is completely the opposite. You are given time to think, time to find out who you are and where you want to be. You are allowed the freedom to be yourself.

I can never thank Janice and Norman enough. They saved my life. Their time, care, support and love will never be forgotten. Without them and The Well Head Centre I would have been dead. They have given me my life back. The most precious gift in the world and I will be forever grateful.

An update from Julia...

I always believed in God, but when I heard people's testimonies, I never believed it until it happened to me!

Whilst I was at The Well Head Centre, as you know I went in to The Healing Rooms for some prayer. I was given some scripture verses which were exactly for my situation. I was prayed for the Hepatitis C which I was diagnosed with. I couldn't believe it when I went for my hospital appointment two weeks later. When I got the blood test results back, they couldn't detect it. The previous appointment said it was aggressive. The nurse was in total shock! It was at that point that I knew it was God. I had to continue to go each day for more tests. I was feeling so much better in myself. Last month I got the confirmation I needed. I was given the all clear. Since then, there have been several situations where I know God has been there for me. My life has changed and a miracle happened. I am completely cured.

The day that I left The Well Head Centre I was very nervous and worried as I felt so safe and secure there. Janice and Norman assured me that I would be fine, as God was with me. They were right. Looking back, I can see that now. My life has completely changed and all for the better.

I have changed as a person. I attend church as often as I can with my shift patterns at work. I am looking forward to going on Alpha and also getting baptised as soon as I can. I am no longer isolated. I attend Life Group each week when I can and I can finally say I am happy with life. What sticks in my mind is the fact that my family now say they have got their daughter back. They can see life back in my eyes again. I am off all the medication I was taking. I never thought that was even a possibility! The Doctors are all shocked at my transformation. The Well Head Centre changed my life. I have formed amazing friendships and have the help, love and support I need from them. I have learned how to deal with my feelings in a positive way.

I am back at work and studying, doing a course on Mental Health, so one day I can be of help to others with similar struggles. Most importantly I believe in myself again and have become a better person. I am able to see light instead of darkness. Feel love instead of hate and I hope that my testimony will one day help someone experience the same.

Testimony 2 – (L) Name withheld.

One day my husband was suddenly and unexpectedly taken very ill and in short, the impact was explosive. Overnight our family's life changed – I became a full-time carer. I felt like a single parent and friends and careers disappeared. I paid privately to see a therapist who listened whilst I talked, cried and generally broke down. After some months my therapist became worried about my wellbeing and referred me to The Well Head Centre. I was so nervous that first day but equally couldn't wait to get away and escape what my daily life had become. Within minutes of being greeted by Janice and Norman I felt like a weight of daily responsibility was lifted from my shoulders. I cried and talked whilst Norman listened and never judged. I slept that first night through to lunch time the next day and awoke feeling lighter. I was responsible only for myself at The Well Head Centre and there were no expectations on me. They offer 'time and space', but much more than that, they offer a welcoming, safe environment with the opportunity to just be. I rested, I read, I walked, I explored and pleased only myself – it may sound selfish but it was the first time since everything happened that I could think about what I needed.

The time and space allowed me to recharge and gain back perspective ready to go back to the responsibilities in my family.

Happily, we are now two years down the line, have a much healthier perspective on life and work, spend much more time together as a family (which the children really enjoy and appreciate) are both well and have new jobs and a brighter future. I cannot speak highly enough of The Well Head Centre, and especially Janice and Norman. What they have created and offer is a place of unconditional, non-judgmental and caring support. Going there saved me!

Testimony 3 – Connie

I came to The Well Head Centre in September last year following a referral from a member of our local church, because I was in desperate need of a retreat.

I am a mum of three children and had been married for nine years at the time. I had been struggling with depression since the birth of our first child. Three years later our twins arrived and it was about a year after I returned to work that we decided that I give up work, for financial reasons, but also because I was physically, mentally and spiritually drained. After around three months I missed my job because I loved it and was good at it. I felt resentful about my situation, I felt lost and worthless, my depression deteriorated and this resentment filtered through into our marriage.

Instead of sharing my feelings with my husband I confided in an old friend from my youth, and over time a relationship developed which lead to my husband and I becoming more and more detached from each other to the point that at the end of our holiday together I told my husband that I wanted to leave him. At the same time, I struggled hugely with the implications of this. I did not want to leave my children and really did not want to subject them to the pain and trauma of a separation.

At this point I realised that I needed a complete 'time out' from MY life. Time to think, consider my options and just have a total break. And this is what The Well Head Centre provides . . . an oasis in our busy, crazy, hectic, demanding lives - run lovingly by Janice and

Norman and their team of dedicated volunteers. Janice and Norman took me in for six days, and I mean, they TOOK me in. We shared meals together, laughter, tears and many, many conversations, and absolutely no obligations or expectations were placed upon me, I was in total control of my time at the Centre, which was EXACTLY what I needed. No judgement was passed at what had happened, or the thoughts I was sharing, just pure love, support and gentle guidance from their wisdom and admiringly deep conviction as Christians. Janice, Norman and the volunteers all act entirely selfless in order to help their residents to find their answers themselves – at least this is how it worked for me. They also helped me to recover spiritually; I decided to hand myself over to God in that week and to accept that my path in life has been determined, to give up the constant need for control and to have faith in His guidance – what a relief!

My stay at the Centre was free of charge. It is run as a charity and therefore funded through donations and other means.

Before I forget - I returned home to my husband a day earlier than planned. We held each other for ages, we both cried for ages with relief and hope, tears of apologies and tears of forgiveness. And then we talked. We have now completed six months' worth of marriage counselling which has been hugely beneficial, and both my husband and I would go as far as saying that my time at The Well Head Centre saved our marriage.

Testimony 4 – Lynda

I was referred to The Well Head Centre in April of 2019. I had been to the Healing Rooms, which shares the building with The Well Head Centre, many years ago when it was first running. But when I was referred, I had no idea it was in the same place. I arrived on the Monday afternoon and met Norman and Janice. I arrived broken, fragmented and badly battered. Saying I was a mess was a huge understatement. I immediately fell in love with Norman and Janice. Although they didn't understand what I was going through they never stinted with their love and acceptance of me. They worked hard at trying to understand. I had many years of people being disrespectful of me, abandoning me, hurting me, abusing me, using me, so to actually be around people who just accepted me, and treated me with respect was quite new and refreshing for me. I decided to go to the Healing Rooms for prayer, just to see what it was all about.

The week at The Well Head Centre was both very hard and very good. The peace and love in the bungalow was almost tangible, like a warm, comfortable duvet on a cold winter night. Norman and Janice tried hard to understand what I was going through. I'm not sure they fully understood, but they accepted me anyway. They gave me time and love. The week passed too quickly, and it was soon time to go home; something I wasn't looking forward to. I wanted to stay longer. I wanted to stay forever! However, I knew I needed God to heal my mind, body and emotions.

I kept coming back to the Healing Rooms and Janice, Ann and Linda always set aside the time to minister to me and pray for me.

At one point, Janice had to release me because it seemed like I wasn't getting any better. In fact, it looked like I was getting worse! But God prompted her to just love me. And her obedience to the Father had astounding results. I didn't know all this at the time, but suddenly things took a 180° turn, and I started getting healed in leaps and bounds.

Dissociative Identity Disorder only happens when a child of around 4-7 is horribly abused, tortured, traumatised and neglected repeatedly. The child unconsciously creates another being (person, animal, inanimate object, fantasy beast: fairy, dragon etc) to take the abuse so she can survive. Dissociation is a survival mechanism. The child being abused thinks "I can't survive this. I need someone else to take the abuse so I can live".

For the first time in my life, I have silence in my head. I am a whole person. A new chapter in my life has begun, and none of this would have happened if it wasn't for the love that was freely given to me by all the volunteers. I am so grateful that I met them. I feel like the luckiest person on the earth. I am humbled by their love for Jesus and for each other. My journey is not over. In fact, it's just begun and I look forward to what God has in store for me.

Guest feedback

We wanted to let you read some of the feedback we received from our guests and referrers. This is just a fraction of the beautiful words of encouragement they wrote to us. I have a scrapbook full of letters and cards we received over the thirteen years and if I were to write them all for you to read, I would have to write another book!! So here is a small sample.

'Second to None'

'I arrived in anxiety and desperateness but left with calmness and peace. The way the Centre is run more than provided for my needs, the kindness and generosity is second to none!' [Stephie]

'Changed my Life'

'My stay changed my life! It gave me my life back and after so much pain has given me peace, hope and looking forward to my future.' [Julia]

'Space to Think'

'I have had space to think clearly. The volunteers are always around to listen but are happy for us to do our own thing too.' [Hayley]

'Best Present Ever!'

'My visit has been the most impacting time of my life. My first day was my birthday! I received the best present in 59 years!' [John]

'Ready to face the world!'

'I was put at ease immediately. I have slept and completely cleared my head! My shoulders are not heavy anymore and I am ready to face the world!' [Jane]

'Instant sense of belonging'

'I feel refreshed! Such a non-judgmental place that I felt an instant sense of belonging.' [Ann]

'Very impressed'

'I'm very impressed by the setup and facilities. My stay has slowed me down and given me time to think through the issues I am facing in a caring environment. It is the first steps in my healing process.' [Brian]

'A little jewel'

'You really have a little jewel here and it is such a beautiful retreat. My time at the Centre has been a time of reflection and rest. It has given me hope and inspiration. Thank you from the bottom of my heart.' [Lisa]

'A weight has lifted'

'My stay at the Centre helped me in so many ways. I can hardly put in to words the feeling that I have but I feel a weight has lifted and I can breathe easier.' [Faye]

'Easy to talk to'

'My stay gave me the headspace I desperately needed! Everyone was so easy to talk to and friendly.' [Emma]

'First time in years'

'I'm leaving feeling more positive and relaxed for the first time in years. I feel like I'm worth something.' [Vivienne]

'Set up perfectly!'

'It couldn't get any better as it is good to talk! The Centre is peaceful, you feel safe and secure, and are not judged.' [Sue]

'Above and beyond!'

'Nothing further could be done [to make my stay more beneficial] it was all above and beyond. The staff are amazing!' [Vicky]

'Lovely, homely and very clean'

'The Centre is lovely, homely and very clean - lots of things to do here and in the town. My stay gave me support to work things through.' [Cherryl]

'Nice to get away'

'It was nice to get away and have a break from stresses at home.' [Natalie]

'Without judgement or pressure'

'It has changed me beyond what I could ever think imaginable in a week! I felt that I could talk freely and listened to in such an understanding way without judgement or pressure.' [Mel]

'Unbelievable!'

'It is unbelievable that there is a place like this!' [Florance]

'Forever thankful'

'I was in such a dark lonely place when I came in and you have helped me see life in a new light. I will be forever thankful.' [Vicky]

'A breath of fresh air!'

'My stay at the Centre was a breath of fresh air when I felt stagnant! I was done with everything ... but being here has given me strength.' [Bethany]

'Wonderful facilities and wonderful people'

'My stay gave me time and space to be in my own company and really think about things!' [Pippa]

'It broke the cycle

'My time at the Centre broke the cycle of pressure and not seeing beyond my immediate surroundings.' [Martin]

'Battery recharged'

'I arrived physically and mentally exhausted and am going home with my battery recharged! The facilities were excellent ...... everything I needed.' [George]

'Most amazing'

'Probably the most amazing experience of my life!' [Andrea]

'What more can one want'

'What more can you want when peace, love, joy and hope reside within these walls! A refuge from life's storms.' [Margaret]

'Able to be me!'

'My stay provided a place and space in which I was able to be and connect with 'me.' [Andy]

'A very calm and loving place'

'The time I spent with you helped me to open up and regain control of my life' [Dawn]

'If you could bottle it'

'If you could bottle what you gain from being here you could help all your mental health problems whenever you needed to. That's how powerful this place is.' [Jade]

'Right place at the right time'

'The week I stayed here felt like I was in the right place at the right time. Whether I was sat in the communal area, my bedroom or going out for a walk I was feeling that being here was giving me space to heal.' [David]

FEEDBACK FROM REFERRERS

'Well-being is so Important'

'I have had the pleasure of meeting Janice and Norman this afternoon to find out about the Centre. A lovely, tranquil place and such caring people. Mental health and well-being is so important and I cannot commend them enough for the generosity of their time and care.' [Rhonda – National Farmers' Union]

'Positive impact'

'A huge thank you for all that you do for the clients we refer to you. From the feedback they give us and the changes we see in them after they have stayed with you, we 100% know that the positive impact The Well Head Centre has on them is immense! Keep up the great work!' [NW Counselling Hub, Lincoln]

'Huge Turning Point'

'I just want to let you know that you made a huge impression on a client that I referred to you. The stay with you was a huge turning point in that client's life and was such a valuable experience that will impact them, I think, for the rest of their life.' [Jo – Counsellor]

Conclusion

When I started journaling back in 2008, little did I think that it would, or even could, be made into a book that someone might like to read!

I hope and pray that you have been inspired to follow your dreams and take the first steps and see what God will do. I had no qualifications, no money and no building to start on this journey but I just knew in my spirit that I was to go down this path. I won't say it was all easy as you have read! All I can say is that it is all worth it. When you get confirming words along the way it sure helps. When you have a faithful prayer team, then that helps too. When you have people who are on board with your dream/vision, that definitely helps. As you have read, it took fifteen years to come into being. All I know is that I believe it was all in God's timing and not mine! May I encourage you to take the first steps and see what happens. If it is of God, then it will continue to gain momentum. If it is not, then it may just fizzle out. Doors that need to be opened will open for you. Those that need to be kept shut will be closed. Whichever, you will have tried. God will reward you for your efforts. It's all good fun and exciting to be in God's plan.

I most certainly want to thank my Father God for His goodness, His provision and His faithfulness all through these last thirteen years. I would not have been able to do any of it without Him. I give Him all the glory, honour and praise for all the lives He has transformed.

With God, there are no endings, just beginnings. So I am now excited and looking forward to this new season. You could say I am just waiting – again!

In memory of

Mary Bull – A faithful friend who was with us from the beginning when it was just a seed in my spirit. She gave of her time and prayerful support even though she was not well. She planned to be my secretary, bless her. She passed away just before we officially opened in 2011.

Natalie Adams – A faithful friend who also was with us from the beginning and supported us in prayer and then passed away just before we opened.

Pete Kelly – A faithful and dedicated volunteer and friend who came nearly every Tuesday for two years to paint and repair things for us in the bungalow right up to us opening and beyond.

Tricia Smith – A faithful friend who supported us financially and in prayer from the very start of the project 'til she passed away 2020. Forever in our prayers.

I shall be forever grateful for all they contributed to make this dream a reality.

Photos

Front door

before

after

Driveway

before

after

Bathroom

Shower room

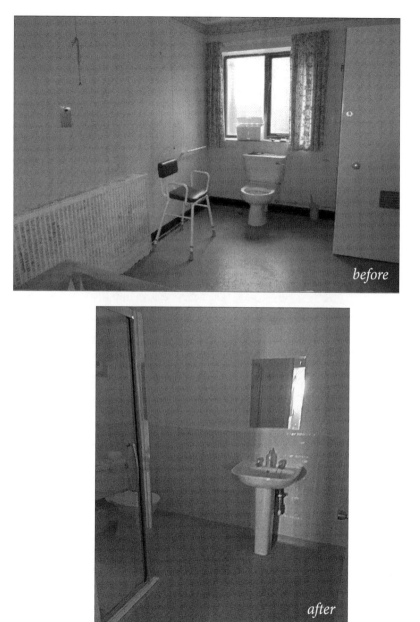

before

after

Office

before

after

Laundry room

Lounge

Bedroom

before

after

Quad area